The Printer's Craft

The Printer's Craft

An Exhibition Selected from the

R. R. DONNELLEY & SONS COMPANY COLLECTION

BY JEFFREY ABT

May through September, 1982

The Joseph Regenstein Library · *The University of Chicago*

This publication was made possible in part with funds provided by
The University of Chicago Library Society.

Library of Congress Catalog Card Number: 82-8433

The University of Chicago Library, Chicago 60637

© 1982 by The University of Chicago Library. All rights reserved.
Published 1982
Printed in the United States of America

ISBN 0 943056 00 4

Foreword

When it came time to dissolve its Training Department Library, the R. R. Donnelley & Sons Company decided to donate the books to two libraries, the Newberry Library and the University of Chicago Library, both of which had long-standing interests in the history of printing. It was left to the two institutions to divide the books between them. In deference to the Newberry's notable emphasis on the subject, epitomized by its John M. Wing Foundation on the History of Printing, it was to have first choice. This would enable it to enhance an already highly select concentration of books. In taking second choice, the University Library expected to add books which would support its own wide-ranging interests in printing and the craft's pervasive influence. Unwanted duplication was to be sold, with the income being equally divided between the two libraries for the purpose of supporting future acquisitions. The duplication was sold at auction in 1980 at the Hanzel Galleries of Chicago. The result has been that the University Library was enriched by some 1,200 volumes, a selection of which now make up this exhibition.

The Training Department Library from which these books came was intimately linked to the Donnelley Company's pioneering commitment to apprentice training and a desire to maintain a tradition of quality as well as the efficient practice of the craft. With a stress on classroom instruction, closely supervised on-the-job training, and access to a well-stocked library, the Donnelley program represented a high point in industrial training in the United States. From 1908, when the apprentice training program was inaugurated, books were acquired to enlarge upon the practical work within the plant as well as illustrate its historical-aesthetic background. Thus there were manuals, textbooks, specimen books, treatises, journals, and other similar works on such fundamental elements of printing as typesetting, composition, presswork, engraving, photography, binding, and design. To enliven the perspective of these day-to-day skills, historical examples of printing craftsmanship were also selectively acquired. These examples included the work of master printers and designers, past and present, plus unusual works which depict innovative applications of the various graphic processes. To these were added various types of printed ephemera illustrating solutions to particular contemporary printing and design problems.

The rapid, almost unbelievable, technological changes in the creation and transmission of print have removed the Donnelley books from any current practical application. The books, however, remain as important historical sources and as artifacts of enduring aesthetic value. They not only embody the past technical side of a craft and an industry but also social, economic, and aesthetic issues which give printing history its special character.

It is the purpose of this exhibition and catalogue to present an overview of the Donnelley Collection. Mr. Jeffrey Abt, Exhibitions Coordinator for the University Library, has been responsible for developing this view by writing the catalogue, supervising its design, and creating the exhibition. Through his efforts it is hoped that our viewers and readers will gain an appreciation of the books and their position in a complex and colorful history.

The exhibition and this catalogue also give the University of Chicago an opportunity to express to the R. R. Donnelley & Sons Company its gratitude for this important addition to its scholarly resources.

ROBERT ROSENTHAL
Curator of Special Collections

Some Finely Printed Books

Introduction

The R. R. Donnelley & Sons Collection is made up of two parts, one consisting of finely printed books, the other, of books on printing and design. Included in the first section are a small number of books issued by leading printers and type designers dating from the early sixteenth to the mid-nineteenth centuries. This section also includes a much larger number of books printed from the late nineteenth century to the present with emphasis on the modern fine printing movement around the turn of the century in England, America, and Germany. The materials in the second part of the collection, ranging from technical manuals and trade periodicals to printed ephemera, illustrate changing technologies and styles in commercial printing from the early nineteenth century until now. *The Printer's Craft* follows this organization, placing books chosen for their fine printing in the first half of the exhibition, and materials on printing and design in the second half.

There are three steps in the printing of a book. First is the design and then the placement, or setting of the type; second, the arrangement of titles, illustrations, and columns of text on the page, called layout or format; and last, the presswork, the actual printing of the book. A finely printed book is one in which the elements of its design—type, illustration, ornament, and layout—are combined in stylistic harmony and printed flawlessly.

The selections of fine printing which follow are arranged chronologically without attempting to present a history of the craft. Instead, they have been chosen to illustrate the aesthetic and technical problems of printing as dealt with by prominent printers and designers from the early sixteenth to the twentieth centuries. Several works, such as John Baskerville's monumental *Holy Bible* or Charles St. John Hornby's *Tutte le opere di Dante*, are landmarks of fine printing. Others, including John Pine's unusual engraved text or Lucien Pissarro's colorful recreation of sixteenth-century musical notation, are selected to throw light on some less familiar aspects of the craft.

Printing began as both an art and a child of the marketplace. From the outset, most printers were required to sacrifice quality to meet economic demands. Printing as an art was cultivated by a small number of printers whose survival was not dependent on profit. These printers, whether with royal patronage or private means, could linger over questions of style and afford to discard a defectively printed sheet. Many of the following books were created under these ideal circumstances and have become, for commercial as well as private printers today, standards of fine printing.

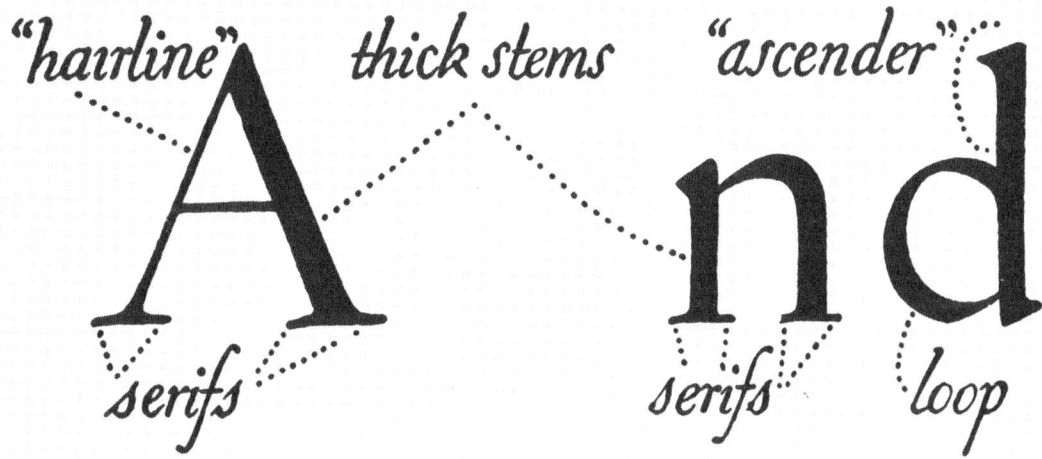

This drawing, illustrating the structure of roman letter design, is enlarged from William A. Dwiggins's *Mss. by WAD*, published by The Typophiles in 1947. It is intended to acquaint the reader with descriptive terminology used in the exhibition text.

The bracketed numbers within the text refer to the bibliographic descriptions and plates illustrating materials shown in the exhibition.

Aldus · Garamond · Pine

The invention of movable type in the mid-fifteenth century took place within a vital scribal tradition. Thus, the success of the nascent craft of printing depended not only on the developing economy of the printed book, but also on the ability of the earliest printers to sustain the familiar appearance of handwritten manuscripts. A major contribution to this effort was the innovation by Aldus Manutius, a Venetian, of the sloping typeface now called italic.

Aldus (1450–1515) combined the erudition of a scholar, the enterprise of a businessman, and the keen eye of a craftsman. His italic, shown here in a 1502 edition of works by the Roman poet Statius, was based on a hand used in the papal chancery for official documents. In addition to its popularity as an accurate imitation of chancery script, italic was also useful to Aldus because it compressed easily into another of his creations, the low-cost, small-format book. These books, when printed with italic type, could carry as much text as larger books set in roman type. This was possible because the italic adopted from its model over sixty pairs of "tied" or connected letters called ligatures. One example is *Et*, condensed into the symbol *&* which is commonly used today as an ampersand. Aldus, following chancery manuscript form, capitalized his italic with roman letters. Italic capitals would not be designed until some fifty years after his death. [1] This edition also includes an orthography of proper names rendered in Greek by one of Aldus's editors. The fine but irregular Greek type used to print the list was modeled after the editor's hand. [2]

By the early sixteenth century the rapid diffusion of printing throughout Europe led to a demand for specialized supporting craftsmen. One of the first groups of specialists to appear was the typefounders, who included among their small number the Frenchman Claude Garamond.

His Majesty Francis I noted the skill of Garamond (ca. 1500–1561) when, in 1540, he sold several fonts of type to Robert Estienne, the Royal Printer. The following year Garamond was asked by the monarch to design and cut a Greek type for the exclusive use of the Royal Printer. The type, designed after the handwriting of Francis I's Greek scribe, was used by Estienne's son Henri in the latter's *Poëtae Graeci principes*, printed in 1566 and opened here to Homer's *Iliad*. Garamond's meticulous renderings skillfully capture the fluid, loping character of the original handwriting heightened with swelling, calligraphic lines. The cursive style of the type is in sharp contrast to Aldus's Greek font but is very close in conception to the latter's italic, particularly in Garamond's use of numerous two- and three-letter ligatures. [3]

With only the rarest of exceptions, texts were printed with movable type from the late fifteenth to the beginning of the nineteenth centuries. John Pine deviated from the norm when he hand engraved the entire text of his illustrated edition of Horace's *Opera*.

Pine (1690–1756), an English artist and engraver, issued the first of two volumes of Horace's poems in 1733, engraved letter by letter on copper plates, a separate plate for each of the over five hundred pages of the

1,2. Publius Papinius Statius. *Statii sylvarum libri quinque Thebaidos libri duodecim Achilleidos duo.* Venice: Aldus Manutius, 1502. Type designed and cut by Francesco Griffo; book design by Aldus Manutius. 16 × 10 cm.

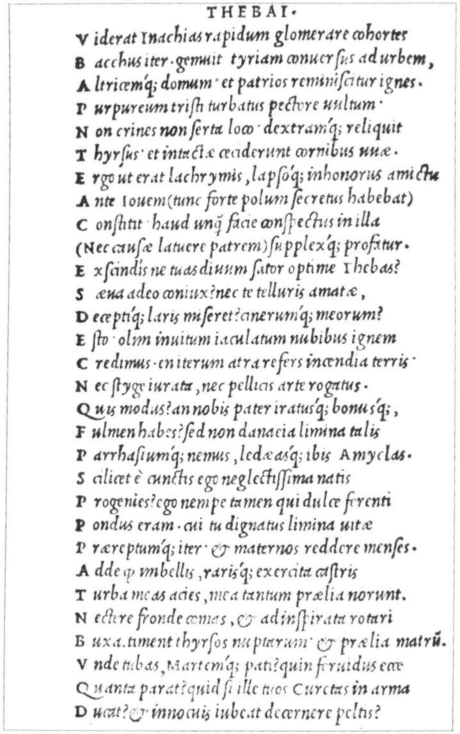

Aldus · Garamond · Pine

THEBAI.

V iderat Inachias rapidum glomerare cohortes
B acchus iter, gemuit tyriam conuersus ad urbem,
A ltricemq; domum et patrios reminiscitur ignes.
P urpureum tristi turbatus pectore uultum
N on crines non serta loco, dextramq; reliquit
T hyrsus, et intactæ cœciderunt cornibus uuæ.
E rgo ut erat lachrymis, lapsoq; inhonorus amictu
A nte Iouem (tunc forte polum secretus habebat)
C onstitit, haud unq̃ facie conspectus in illa
(Nec causæ latuere patrem) supplexq; profitur.
E x scindis ne tuas diuum sator optime Thebas?
S æua adeo coniux? nec te telluris amatæ,
D eceptiq; laris miseret? anerumq; meorum?
E sto olim inuitum iaculatum nubibus ignem
C redimus, en iterum atra refers incendia terris.
N ec stygi iurata, nec pellicis arte rogatus.
Q uis modas? an nobis pater iratusq; bonusq;,
F ulmen habes? sed non danaeia limina talis
P arrhasiumq; nemus, ledæasq; ibis Amyclas.
S alicet è cunctis ego neglectissima natis
P rogenies? ego nempe tamen qui dulce ferenti
P ondus eram, cui tu dignatus limina uitæ
P ræreptumq; iter, & maternos reddere menses.
A dde q̃ imbellis, rarisq; exercita castris
T urba meas acies, mea tantum prælia norunt.
N ectere fronde comas, & adinstirata rotari
B uxa, timent thyrsos nuptarum, & prælia matrũ.
V nde tubas, Martemq; pati? quin fœtidus ecce
Q uantæ parat? quid si ille tuos Curetas in arma
D ucat? & innocuis iubeat decernere peltis?

PLATE 1

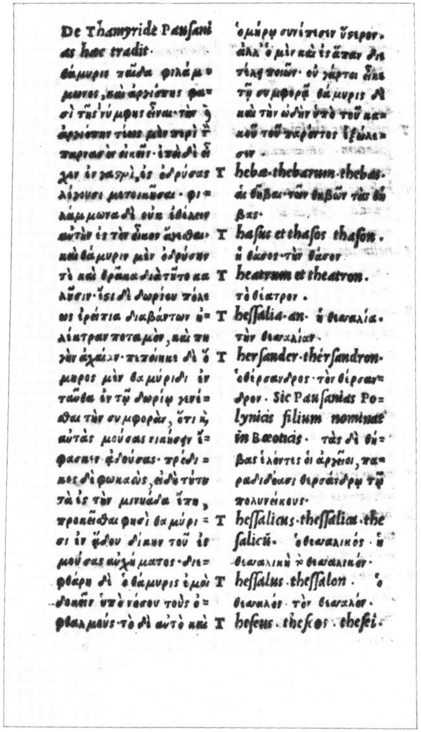

PLATE 2

completed work. The lettering was probably modeled after a contemporary French typeface, particularly the vertical stresses on lowercase a's, r's, s's, and the lofty dots over the i's. But Pine, following his instincts as an engraver, incised the serifs and hairlines (on uppercase N's, for instance) with extremely fine lines. The result is a striking contrast between the thin hairlines and long and equally thin serifs on the one hand, and the heavy stems on the other. This epigraphic look, recalling the style of Roman inscriptions, suits the illustrations and may have influenced type designers later in the eighteenth century. [4, 5 left] Pine's tech-

3. *Poëtae Graeci principes heroici carminis, & alii nonnulli.* [Geneva:] Henry Estienne II, 1566. Type designed and cut by Claude Garamond. 35.8 × 22.3 cm.

4,5. Horace. *Opera.* London: John Pine, 1733–1737. Illustrations, initials, lettering, and book design by John Pine. 23.5 × 15 cm.

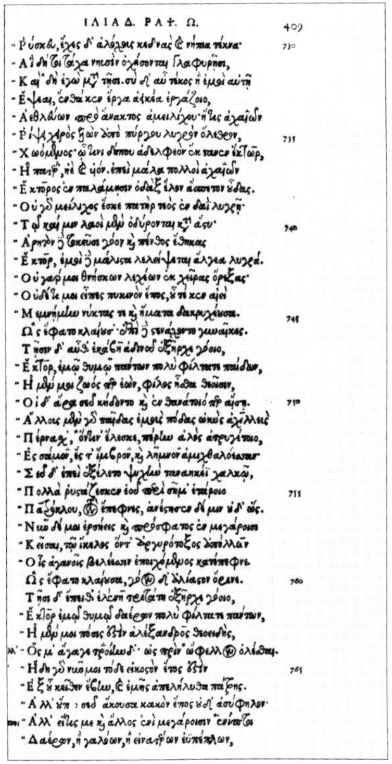

PLATE 3

18 Q. HORATII FLACCI

ODE X.
HYMNVS IN MERCVRIVM.

MERCVRI facunde, nepos Atlantis,
Qui feros cultus hominum recentum
Voce formasti catus, et decorae
    More palaestrae:
Te canam, magni Iovis et Deorum   5
Nuncium, curvaeque lyrae parentem;
Callidum, quidquid placuit, jocofo
    Condere furto.
Te, boves olim nisi reddidisses
Per dolum amotas, puerum minaci   10
Voce dum terret, viduus pharetra
    Risit Apollo.
Quin et Atridas, duce te, superbos,
Ilio dives Priamus relicto,
Thessalosque ignes, et iniqua Trojae   15
    Castra fefellit.

CARMINVM LIBER I. 19

Tu pias laetis animas reponis
Sedibus; virgaque levem coerces
Aurea turbam, superis Deorum
    Gratus, et imis.   20

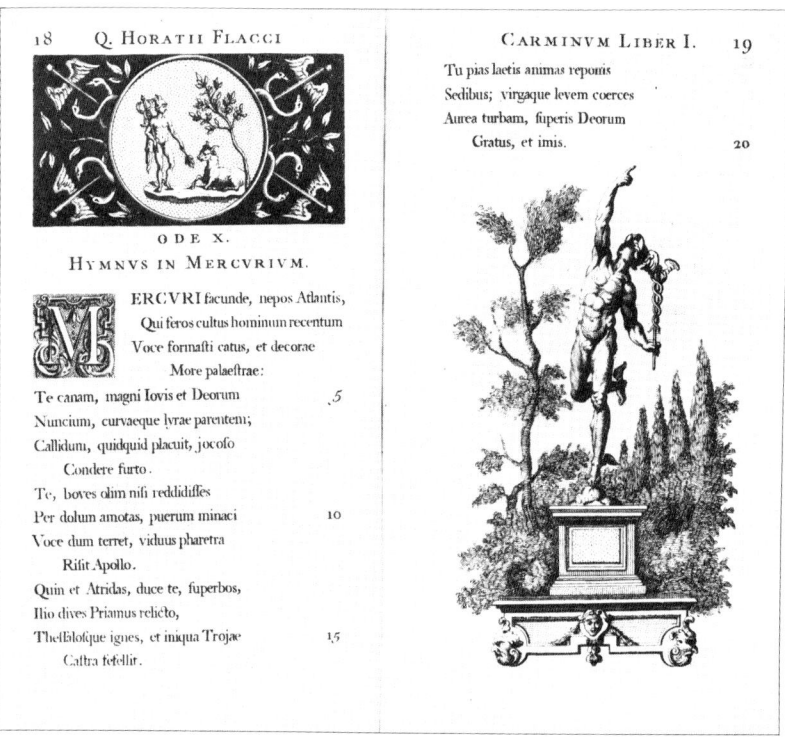

PLATE 4

manae imago, tanquam in speculo exhibetur, quam tibi ineunte aetate tua convenire potest? Nam hinc diversos hominum mores, nec minus diversos exitus, quo virtus, quo vitium ferat, pariter edisces; pulchraque illa instituta, quibus viri illustrissimi STEPHANI POYNTZ ductu et consiliis ad veram gloriam dudum instructus es, facili negotio in mentem revocabis. Vt in dies autem omni laude TANTI PRINCIPIS fastigio digna magis cumulatus adolescas, et spes optimas, quas pridem de te gens Britannica concepit, non aeques modo, sed etiam superes, cum omnibus bonis enixe orat precaturque

Johannes Pine.

SUBSCRIBERS.

The King.
S. M. I. L'Empereur des Romains.
S. M. I. L'Impératrice.
Le Roy de France.
Le Roy d'Espagne.
La Reine d'Espagne.
Le Roy de Portugal.
S. A. R. le Grand Duc de Tuscane.
Her Royal Highness the Princess of Wales.
S. A. R. M.gr le Prince des Asturies.
S. A. R. M.me la Princesse des Asturies.

PLATE 5

nique also enabled him to copy cursive handwriting by connecting all the letters of a word, and with a convincing flair impossible with movable type. [5 right]

This method also facilitated Pine's integration of text and illustration on the same page. For the conclusion of "Hymnus in Mercurium," Pine arranged his lettering around the image toward the head of the page, bracketing the whole with the running title at the top and the cut-away base of the sculpture on the bottom. A smokey residue of ink has been left on the upper half of the plate which, along with Pine's delicately suggested clouds, merges the two disparate elements of letter forms and illustration into a unified image. [4 right]

Baskerville · Bodoni · Whittingham & Pickering

By the middle of the eighteenth century the manuscript tradition, which once inspired earlier generations of type and book designers, had virtually disappeared. In its place a number of printers began to design new typefaces which reflected a taste for the lighter, erect forms of Roman epigraphy. Two printers who led the movement away from manuscript letter forms to a more inscriptional style were John Baskerville and Giambattista Bodoni.

John Baskerville (1706–1775) first worked as a writing master in Birmingham before gaining financial success manufacturing lacquerware. However it was not until 1751 that Baskerville, dismayed by the low standards of English typography and printing, and fulfilling an interest held since his youth, started to design type. His press became celebrated for its distinctive type as well as the finish of its spare, unadorned books.

Baskerville's most ambitious undertaking, a folio Bible, was announced in 1757, though not completed until 1763. The sizable format of the volume enabled Baskerville to use a large-scale version of his type which shows more clearly how he crystallized the bold contrast of thin hairlines and heavy stems found in Pine's Horace, with which Baskerville was well acquainted. In addition, Baskerville has set the type with wide spacing, or "leading," between the lines to lighten the appearance, creating an open and delicate lace-work effect. The luster of the pages was achieved by literally ironing the printed sheets with heated metal plates to eradicate the subtle relief which results from printing with movable type. This preference for polished surfaces is probably carried over from Baskerville's japanning business in which the final rubbing of the lacquered surface is so important in eliminating blemishes and deepening the finish. [6]

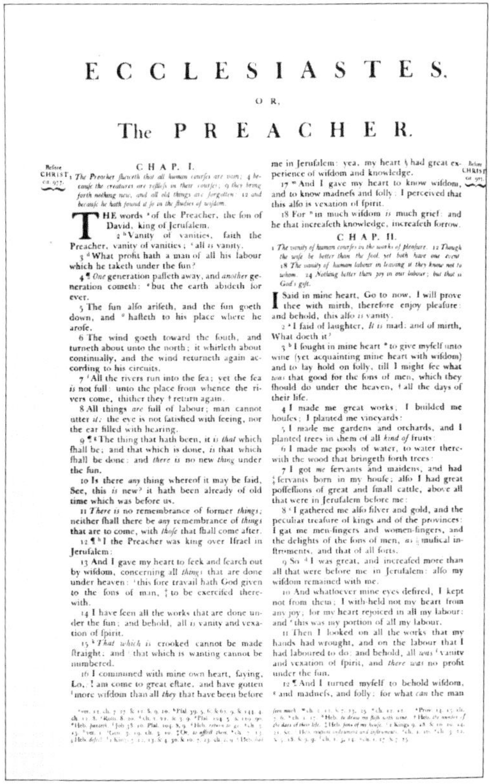

Having apprenticed with his father, Giambattista Bodoni (1740–1813) subsequently traveled to Rome where he refined his skills as a typographer in a papal printing office. In 1768, Bodoni was invited to manage the Duke of Parma's press where he was given a free hand to pursue his fastidious typography and presswork. Bodoni succeeded in setting a high standard for his contemporaries as well as attracting to the ducal palace the kind of prestige brought to the court of Versailles by its Imprimerie Royale.

This edition of poetry by the fifteenth-century Italian poet and scholar Angelo

PLATE 6

6. *The Holy Bible.* Cambridge: John Baskerville, 1763. Type and book design by John Baskerville. Edition: 1250. First subscriber list. 50 × 33 cm.

Poliziano is set in "Testo Acqui." It is one of several of Bodoni's almost imperceptible variations on his basic roman typeface in which he exaggerated the contrast between his razor-thin serifs and weighty stems. Further, the inner surfaces of the stems of lowercase o's, f's, c's, and n's, which in earlier typefaces were allowed to swell and taper calligraphically, are squared by Bodoni. This amounts to a denial of the manuscript origins of the roman letter form and results in a very regular, virtually mechanical appearance. While Bodoni's letter spacing suggests that of Baskerville, Bodoni widens the spaces between letters to the point that words nearly break down into individual letters, particularly words set entirely in uppercase. Bodoni achieved the

7. Angelo Poliziano. *Le stanze di Messer Angelo Poliziano di nuovo pubblicate.* Parma: Nel Regal Palazzo, 1792. Type and book design by Giambattista Bodoni. 31.3 × 23.5 cm.

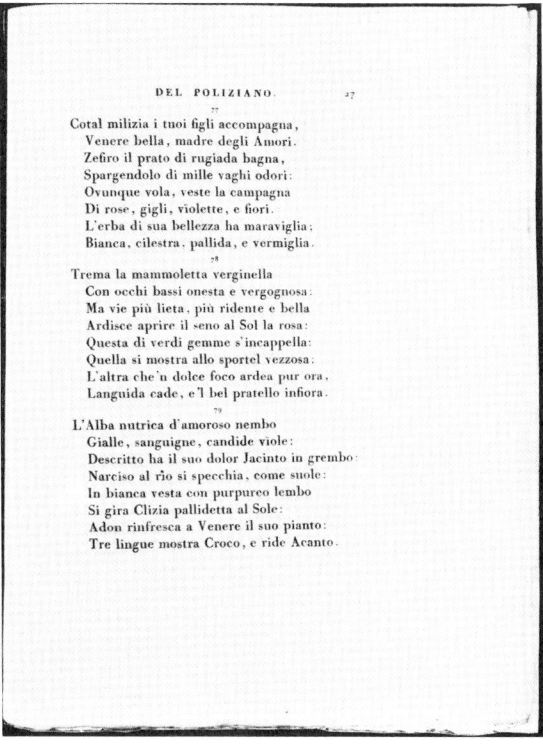

PLATE 7

typographic purity he sought, but not without creating a machined typography and sanitized presswork that can often appear icy and uninviting. [7]

Among the major technological advances of the nineteenth century was the replacement of hand presses with steam-powered equipment. For some printers, this transition to mechanized processes meant a temporary decline in workmanship and made the aesthetics of type and book design minor issues. For others, including the two Englishmen Charles Whittingham II and William Pickering, this became a time for reassessing and improving the appearance of books based on the study of earlier book designs and typefaces.

Whittingham (1795–1876) apprenticed in printing with his uncle Charles Whittingham I and eventually took over the latter's prestigious Chiswick Press. The younger Whittingham, respected for his innovative book designs and impeccable craftsmanship, moved to London in 1828 where he met Pickering (1796–1854), an enterprising and imaginative bookseller who occasionally published fine editions. Specializing in the antiquarian book trade, Pickering brought ideas for the design of their joint ventures derived from his stock of early printed books. Their common admiration of the work of earlier printers led directly to the recovery and recasting of several typefaces first cut nearly one hundred years earlier by the English typefounder William Caslon. One, an English black letter, is shown here in an 1844 edition of the *Book of Common Prayer*. The angular, essentially Gothic style of the type does not quite fit the Victorian delicacy of the initials and ornaments, themselves based on early sources. But the type, crisply set in regular lines and precisely justified columns, blends into plaited tapestries that have their own ornamental effect. The use of red titles or rubrications is drawn from a tradition which began in the fifteenth century and became most common in seventeenth-century printing on the Continent. [8]

8. *The Book of Common Prayer.* London: William Pickering, 1844. Initials and ornaments designed by Mary Byfield; typefounder, William Caslon; book design by Charles Whittingham II; printed by Chiswick Press. 36 × 24.5 cm.

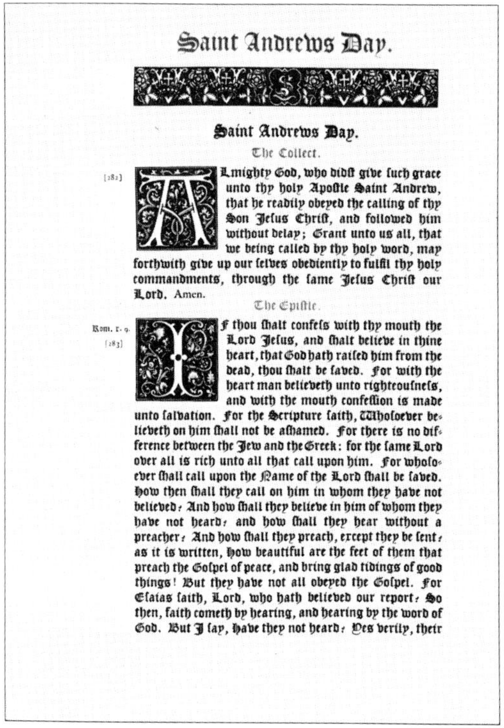

PLATE 8

Morris · The Kelmscott Press

William Morris, believing that "a work of utility might also be a work of art," attempted to restore to the design and printing of books a material integrity and stylistic unity which he felt had been gradually slipping away since the fifteenth century.

While studying for the ministry at Oxford, Morris (1834–1896) embraced a romantic theory which attributed the splendor of Gothic art and architecture to the skill and devotion of the medieval guildsman. Morris believed that the uplifting nature of the guildsman's work as a craftsman imbued the products of his hands with a spirited design and high quality lacking in the mechanically produced goods of Morris's time. Further, he believed that if the handcrafts could be revived on a society-wide scale they would lead both to better design and craft in the applied arts, and to economic independence for the exploited laborers of industrialized England. Determined to realize this ideal, Morris forsook his religious vocation in order to combine the life of a consummate decorator-craftsman with work as a socialist organizer.

A prolific author, Morris is supposed to have said as he leafed through a volume printed by Aldus Manutius, that he wished he could have his writings "done so beautifully." But it did not occur to him to design and print his own books until he chanced to help his friend Emery Walker (1851–1933), a typographer, prepare an illustrated lecture on printing. Probing deeper than Pickering and Whittingham, he went back to the fifteenth century to scrutinize the materials, techniques, and designs of incunables and their medieval models. Morris discovered three principles from these investigations which governed his work as a printer: first, the ratio of black to white within and among typographic elements should be balanced, blending into optically uniform patterns; second, facing pages of an open book should be arranged so that they become a single compositional unit; and third, all the components of a book, namely type, initials, ornaments, illustrations, and binding, should be stylistically consistent, and to Morris's taste, Gothic.

The Kelmscott Press, which Morris assembled adjacent to his home, began printing in 1891. Among its earliest issues is *A Dream of John Ball*, printed in 1892, a visual summary of Morris's initial technical and stylistic experiments. The design of his Golden type is based on that of the fifteenth-century Venetian printer Nicolas Jenson, selected for what was, and still is, widely considered one of the most perfectly proportioned letter designs since the invention of movable type. [9] Morris's adaptation nearly erases the usual eighteenth- and nineteenth-century contrast between stems and hairlines. The square shape of the letter, exaggerated by Morris, eliminates the leading required by the attenuated types of Baskerville and Bodoni. Morris could thereby compress the setting of his type both horizontally and vertically, weaving the heavy blacks of the letters and the white background into an integrated, shimmering pattern. Morris rearranged the opening by dropping the running titles to opposite shoulders of the text and by moving the squares of text up and toward the center of the opened book. Each side with its wide left-hand, right-hand, and bottom margins no longer functions as an independent symmetrical unit, but as one half of a balanced whole. The overall stylistic unity of the book is enhanced by the soft vellum binding with silk ties and untrimmed pages which, though unhandy, tend to authenticate this imitation of the fifteenth-century book. [10]

Morris was a supreme designer of ornament, and nowhere is his inventive genius more abundantly evident than in the daz-

9. Diogenes Laertius. *Vitae et sententiae philosophorum.* [Leaf.] Venice: Nicolas Jenson, 1475. Type design by Nicolas Jenson. 28.5 × 20 cm.

10. William Morris. *A Dream of John Ball* and *A King's Lesson.* Hammersmith: Kelmscott Press, 1892. Illustration designed by Edward Burne-Jones; initials, ornaments, type, and book design by William Morris. Edition: 300. 21 × 15 cm.

11. *The History of Reynard the Foxe.* William Caxton's trans. ed. by Henry Halliday Sparling. London: Bernard Quaritch, 1892. Title, initials, ornaments, type, and book design by William Morris; printed by Kelmscott Press. Edition: 300. 29.2 × 21 cm.

PLATE 10

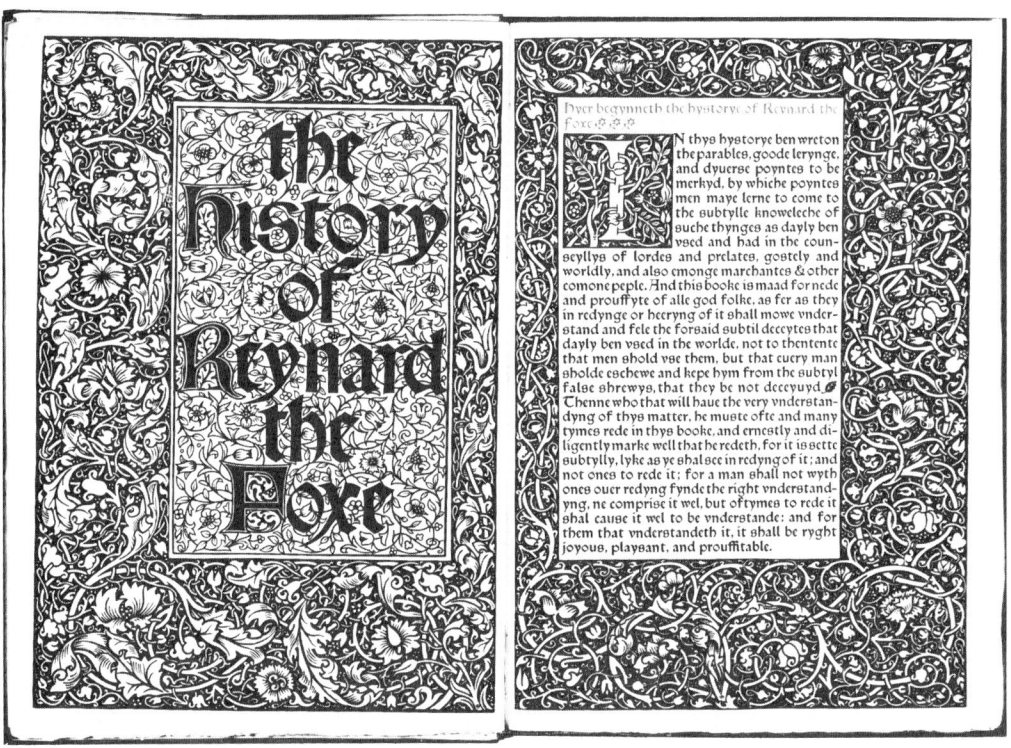

PLATE 11

zling carpet-page openings of his books. In *The History of Reynard the Foxe*, printed in 1892, the two outside white-over-black borders and the initial, though made up of different patterns, balance perfectly in value. And the opening on the right, containing the opening lines of the text set in Morris's Troy type, is matched by the black-over-white filigree background of the title block. The Troy type, which recalls several different fifteenth-century faces, was designed by Morris without reference to a particular model. The undisciplined angularity of the type resists compression, particularly the lopsided lowercase o. The result is a jerky setting in which word and sentence divisions are difficult to discern and the eye is distracted by the irregular shapes of type and punctuation. The pages of this and all subsequent Kelmscott books are trimmed slightly, preserving traces of the deckle edges to capture a hint of the antique without hindering the utility of the book. [11]

Morris's criteria of stylistic and tonal harmony included the use of illustration. One, shown here in *The Story of the Glittering Plain*, completed in 1894, is by Walter Crane (1845–1915), an English illustrator and friend of Morris. The woodcut is tied to the typography through the light areas of hatching picked up by the border ornaments and carried into the fields of type, and through the dark passage of the forest repeated in the large initial below. [12]

All of the Kelmscott titles were printed in small editions which generally included a handful of copies printed on vellum, following the practice of some fifteenth-century printers. The skin provides a smooth, receptive surface for the ink, resulting in

12. William Morris. *The Story of the Glittering Plain*. Hammersmith: Kelmscott Press, 1894. Illustrations designed by Walter Crane; title, initials, ornaments, type, and book design by William Morris. Edition: 250. 29.1 × 21.5 cm.

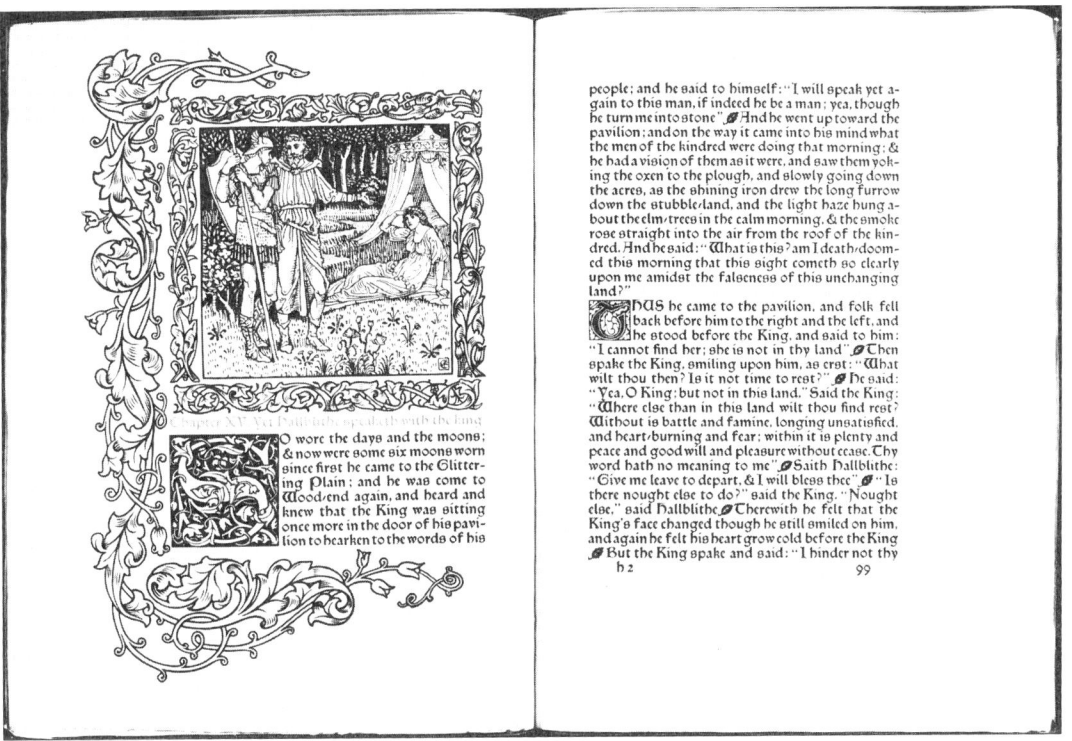

PLATE 12

PLATE 13

sharp, even impressions, as shown in this copy of *Sire Degrevaunt* printed in 1896. There is a magic about vellum books that goes beyond the visual and includes the feel and aroma of the material, an enchantment that lies at the heart of Morris's goal of re-creating the early book in its spiritual as well as material entirety. [13]

13. *Sire Degrevaunt.* Ed. by F. S. Ellis. From edition printed by J. O. Halliwell. Hammersmith: Kelmscott Press, 1896. Illustration designed by Edward Burne-Jones; initials, ornaments, type, and book design by William Morris. One of eight on vellum. 22 × 15 cm.

St. John Hornby · The Ashendene Press

Charles St. John Hornby translated Morris's ideas on book design from the latter's heavy and crowded Gothic style into the spacious, light-filled style of the Renaissance.

A well-educated English businessman, St. John Hornby (1867–1946) began his press as a hobby on the family estate. But a visit by the young, modest novice to the aging but ever-enthusiastic Morris inspired him to raise his sights. Among the first books printed at his Ashendene Press was St. John Hornby's *Ye Minutes*, printed in 1896 with a badly worn font of Caslon roman face, purchased second-hand. But St. John Hornby's quick grasp of the essentials of Morris's teachings is evident in the placement of the running titles at opposite shoulders of the text and the location of the squares of text toward the upper center of the opening. St. John Hornby justifiably fretted over the faint and uneven presswork, and turned his attention to technique. [14]

The full, two-color inking of St. John Hornby's *Boke off the Revelacion*, completed in 1901, reveals a growing mastery of the craft and a taste for the intricate forms of black letter type. An English adaptation of a Dutch face, the type was cut in the seventeenth century for the Printer to the University of Oxford. Lent to St. John Hornby by the University's press, the type enabled him to edge closer to the look of a fifteenth-century text. The arresting yet, in St. John Hornby's word, "clumsy" ini-

14. John Todhunter. *Ye Minutes of Ye CLXXVIIth Meeting of Ye Sette of Odd Volumes, Extracted from Ye Diary of Samuel Pepys.* Hertford: Ashendene Press, 1896. Typefounder, William Caslon; book design by C. H. St. John Hornby. No. 14 of 154. 15 × 12 cm.

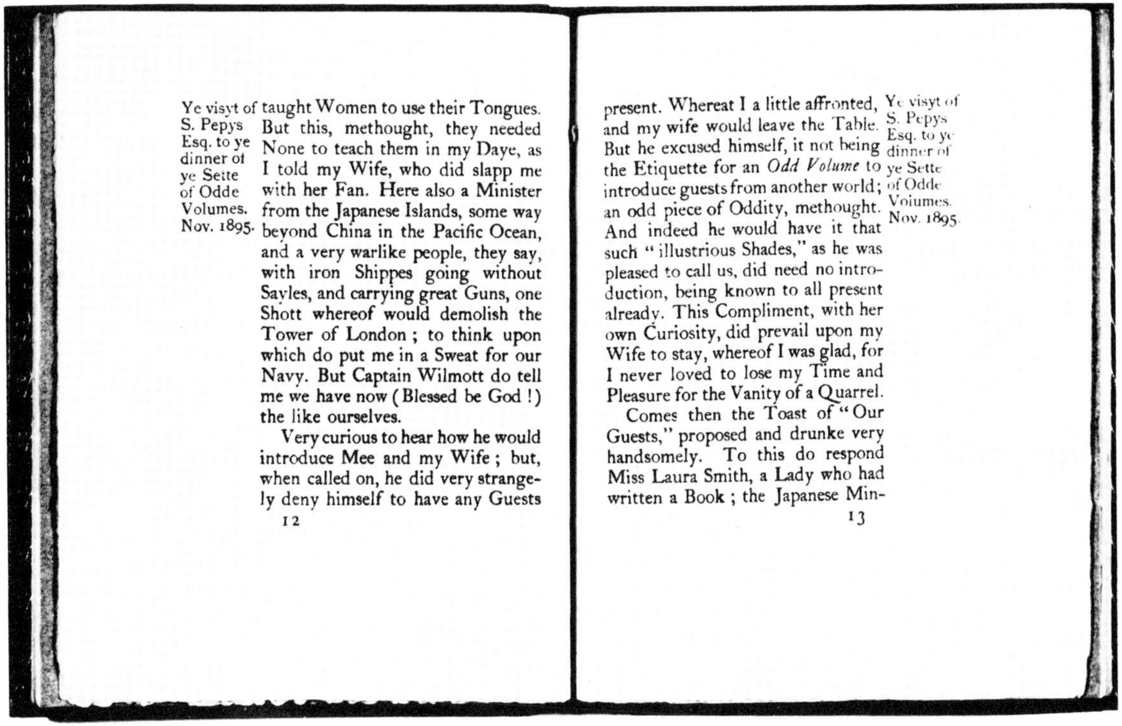

Ye visyt of taught Women to use their Tongues.
S. Pepys But this, methought, they needed
Esq. to ye None to teach them in my Daye, as
dinner of I told my Wife, who did slapp me
ye Sette
of Odde with her Fan. Here also a Minister
Volumes. from the Japanese Islands, some way
Nov. 1895. beyond China in the Pacific Ocean,
and a very warlike people, they say,
with iron Shippes going without
Sayles, and carrying great Guns, one
Shott whereof would demolish the
Tower of London; to think upon
which do put me in a Sweat for our
Navy. But Captain Wilmott do tell
me we have now (Blessed be God!)
the like ourselves.

Very curious to hear how he would
introduce Mee and my Wife; but,
when called on, he did very strange‑
ly deny himself to have any Guests

12

present. Whereat I a little affronted, Ye visyt of
and my wife would leave the Table. S. Pepys
But he excused himself, it not being dinner of
the Etiquette for an *Odd Volume* to ye Sette
introduce guests from another world; of Odde
an odd piece of Oddity, methought. Volumes.
And indeed he would have it that Nov. 1895.
such "illustrious Shades," as he was
pleased to call us, did need no intro‑
duction, being known to all present
already. This Compliment, with her
own Curiosity, did prevail upon my
Wife to stay, whereof I was glad, for
I never loved to lose my Time and
Pleasure for the Vanity of a Quarrel.

Comes then the Toast of "Our
Guests," proposed and drunke very
handsomely. To this do respond
Miss Laura Smith, a Lady who had
written a Book; the Japanese Min‑

13

PLATE 14

Some Finely Printed Books

(Photograph of an opened book showing two pages of blackletter text from Tyndale's New Testament, Revelation chapters 16–17.)

PLATE 15

tials, were designed by him for this his last edition to be set with either a purchased or borrowed type. [15]

Work on St. John Hornby's first "house" type, shown here in a copy of the *Carmina Sapphica* (1903), was begun before the completion of the *Boke*. The idea of a uniquely Ashendene type was suggested by Sydney Cockerell (1867–1962), once secretary to the Kelmscott Press and at the time partner in a typographic engraving firm with Emery Walker. Designed primarily by Walker, the Subiaco type is a marriage of a Gothic type and a Venetian roman face. The spiky stubble has been rounded off the thick stems of the Gothic, and its lanky angularity softened by the gestural, curvilinear influence of the Venetian form. By printing the *Carmina Sapphica* on vellum, St. John Hornby, like Morris, was conjuring up the fifteenth-century book. St. John Hornby went one step further, however, by having the initials penned in by Graily Hewitt (1864–1952), an English calligrapher. [16]

15. *The Boke off the Revelacion off Sanct Jhon the Devine*. Trans. by William Tyndale. Chelsea: Ashendene Press, 1901. Typefounder, Peter De Walpergen [Fell type, Oxford University, Pica black letter]; initials and ornaments by C. H. St. John Hornby. No. 35 of 54. 21.8 × 16.3 cm.

16. Horace. *Carmina Sapphica*. Chelsea: Ashendene Press, 1903. Manuscript initials by Graily Hewitt; type design by Sydney Cockerell and Emery Walker; book design by C. H. St. John Hornby. One of twenty on vellum. 18.5 × 13.1 cm.

17. Dante Alighieri. *Tutte le opere di Dante Alighieri fiorentino*. Ed. by Edward Moore. Chelsea: [Ashendene Press,] 1909. Illustrations designed by Charles M. Gere; initials designed by Graily Hewitt; type design by Sydney Cockerell and Emery Walker; book design by C. H. St. John Hornby. Edition: 105. 42 × 29.2 cm.

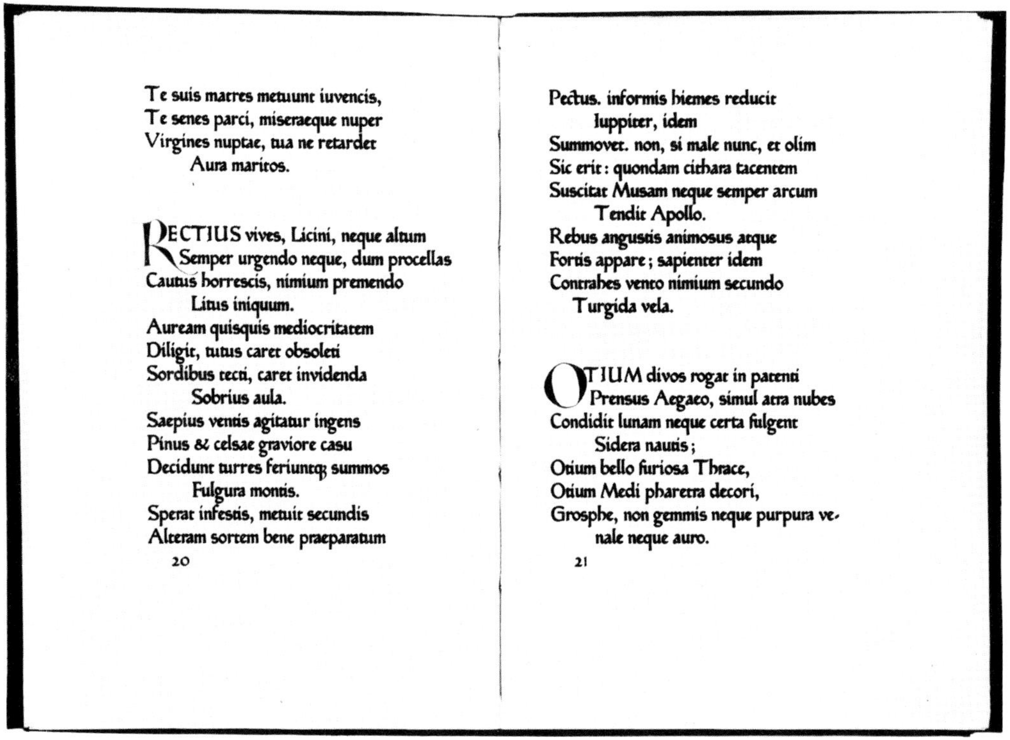

Te suis matres metuunt iuvencis,
Te senes parci, miseraeque nuper
Virgines nuptae, tua ne retardet
    Aura maritos.

RECTIUS vives, Licini, neque altum
Semper urgendo neque, dum procellas
Cautus horrescis, nimium premendo
    Litus iniquum.
Auream quisquis mediocritatem
Diligit, tutus caret obsoleti
Sordibus tecti, caret invidenda
    Sobrius aula.
Saepius ventis agitatur ingens
Pinus & celsae graviore casu
Decidunt turres feriuntq; summos
    Fulgura montis.
Sperat infestis, metuit secundis
Alteram sortem bene praeparatum

Pectus. informis hiemes reducit
    Iuppiter, idem
Summovet. non, si male nunc, et olim
Sic erit: quondam cithara tacentem
Suscitat Musam neque semper arcum
    Tendit Apollo.
Rebus angustis animosus atque
Fortis appare; sapienter idem
Contrahes vento nimium secundo
    Turgida vela.

OTIUM divos rogat in patenti
Prensus Aegaeo, simul atra nubes
Condidit lunam neque certa fulgent
    Sidera nautis;
Otium bello furiosa Thrace,
Otium Medi pharetra decori,
Grosphe, non gemmis neque purpura ve-
    nale neque auro.

PLATE 16

PLATE 17

With the majestic *Tutte le opere di Dante*, completed in 1909, St. John Hornby's independence from Morris was complete. Although faithful to Morris in the overall arrangement of the two-page opening, St. John Hornby differed by abandoning Morris's balanced black-white typographic ratio for a lighter timbre. St. John Hornby's thin inking over the finely textured type and illustration narrows the tonal range of the work to a lighter voice as opposed to Morris's deep, sonorous blacks. The effect of St. John Hornby's light typography and expansive margins is that of bright external illumination, as though viewed in sunlight. St. John Hornby's predisposition toward the uses of blank or "negative" space is important in his placement of the large woodcut, calligraphic-style initials designed by Hewitt. Here the uppercase N is placed within an optical frame defined by the lower edge of the illustration and adjacent lines of type. Morris, by contrast, would have filled the space occupied by the initial with writhing flora. Morris's *horror vacui* has been supplanted by St. John Hornby's acceptance of "negative" space as a positive compositional device. [17]

Cobden-Sanderson & Walker · The Doves Press

Thomas James Cobden-Sanderson and Emery Walker agreed that Morris's books, though beautiful, were so cluttered with distracting ornaments, and the types so muddled, that they were nearly illegible. Cobden-Sanderson and Walker went on to form a partnerhip to create books which were not only readable, but designed to be "beautiful by force of the mere typography" alone.

After a conventional English schooling, Cobden-Sanderson (1840-1922) entered Trinity College, Cambridge, expecting to take holy orders, when a nervous breakdown forced him to abandon his plans. Cobden-Sanderson drifted listlessly for several years looking for a profession that would sustain him materially and spiritually. He found his answer in bookbinding and rapidly acquired the skills to become one of the leading design binders of the time. Still restive, Cobden-Sanderson was not satisfied with interpreting books through their covers alone. He formed a partnership with Emery Walker, and together they founded the Doves Press. Walker brought a sound technical expertise and sober pragmatism to the relationship, which guided the Press into an unrelentingly high standard of craft, while Cobden-Sanderson contributed a fervid vision and missionary intensity. The first issue of the Doves Press was born with a technical maturity and stylistic resolution from which the works that followed would neither deviate nor evolve.

One of the earliest and most ambitious Doves efforts is *The English Bible* (1903–1905). It is set in the Doves type, designed under the supervision of Emery Walker after Jenson. Walker's translation is far more literal than Morris's, however, restoring the pen-like strokes obscured in

36 *Some Finely Printed Books*

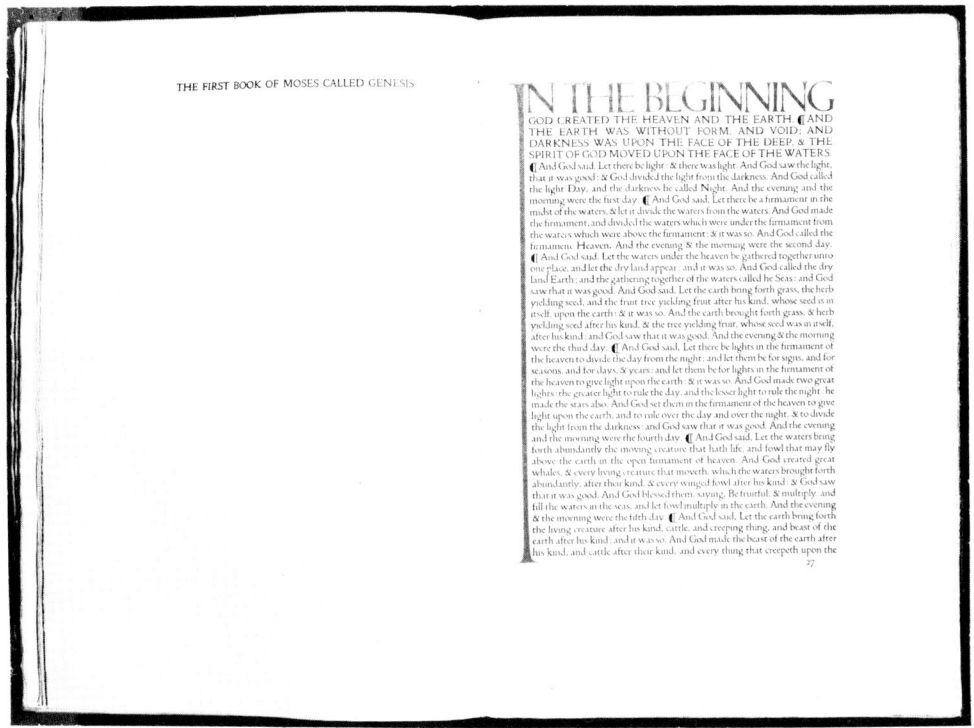

PLATE 18

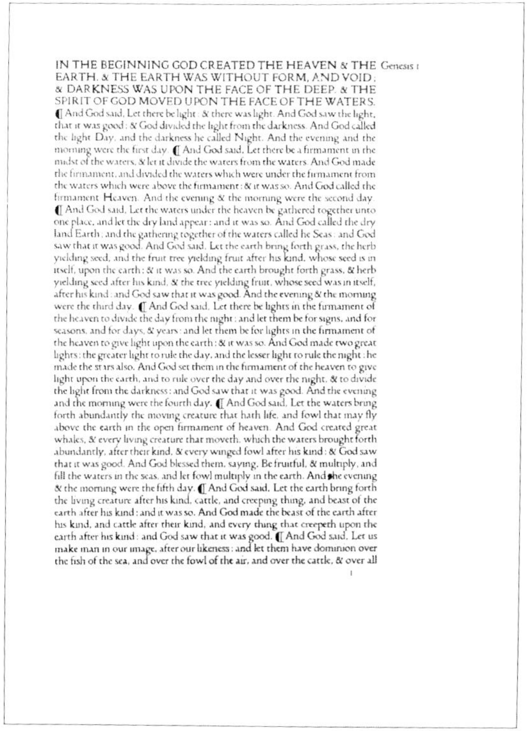

18. *The English Bible*. Ed. by Rev. F. H. Scrivener. Hammersmith: Doves Press, 1903–1905. Initial and leading words by Edward Johnston; type design by Emery Walker; book design by T. J. Cobden-Sanderson and Emery Walker. Edition: 500. 33.8 × 23.5 cm.

19. *The English Bible*. [Specimen page.] Ed. by Rev. F. H. Scrivener. Hammersmith: Doves Press, 1902. Type design by Emery Walker; page design by T. J. Cobden-Sanderson and Emery Walker. Not published as presented. 33 × 23.8 cm.

PLATE 19

Morris's fattened Golden type design. The calligraphic transitions from stem to hairline are necessary to convey the lilting cadence intrinsic to Jenson, especially in the lowercase e's, d's, o's, and p's. Walker has even restored the curious archaism of the wandering dot over the i. The format follows Morris closely; and for the use and placement of the calligraphic initials and leading words, Cobden-Sanderson is indebted to St. John Hornby. The compressed setting, bordering on perfection in the distribution of type and spacing of words and lines, yields a lighter typographic pattern that equals the beauty of Morris's *John Ball*, but with a much improved legibility. [18]

Originally Cobden-Sanderson and Walker planned to issue their *Bible* with a first page set only in Doves type, but Cobden-Sanderson felt that the leading words called for a more impressive opening and created the final design concept. The resulting use of the I running the length of the text block and the calligraphic leading words, transforms what would have been a rather dull design for the first page into one of nobility and grandeur. [19]

The Doves *Sartor Resartus*, finished in 1907, addressed two problems in book design. The first was how to give special emphasis to major book divisions without elaborate ornaments or yawning gaps in the text. Cobden-Sanderson settled on initials placed outside the text. The elegant and monumental initial shown here electrifies the heading without diminishing the epigraphic setting of the opening lines of the text. The second problem recurred fre-

20. Thomas Carlyle. *Sartor Resartus: The Life & Opinions of Herr Teufelsdroeckh*. Hammersmith: Doves Press, 1907. Initials by Edward Johnston; roman type design by Emery Walker; italic typefounder, [Miller & Richard, designed by Alexander Phemister?]; book design by T. J. Cobden-Sanderson and Emery Walker. Edition: 300. 23.9 × 17.2 cm.

BOOK I. CHAPTER I. PRELIMINARY.

CONSIDERING OUR PRESENT ADVANCT STATE OF CULTURE, AND HOW THE TORCH OF SCIENCE HAS NOW BEEN BRANDISHED & BORNE ABOUT, WITH MORE OR LESS EFFECT, FOR 5000 YEARS & upwards; how, in these times especially, not only the Torch still burns, and perhaps more fiercely than ever, but innumerable Rush-lights, and Sulphur-matches, kindled thereat, are also glancing in every direction, so that not the smallest cranny or doghole in Nature or Art can remain unilluminated,—it might strike the reflective mind with some surprise that hitherto little or nothing of a fundamental character, whether in the way of Philosophy or History, has been written on the subject of Clothes. ❡ Our Theory of Gravitation is as good as perfect: Lagrange, it is well known, has proved that the Planetary System, on this scheme, will endure forever; Laplace, still more cunningly, even guesses that it could not have been made on any other scheme. Whereby, at least, our nautical Logbooks can be better kept; & water-transport of all kinds has grown more commodious. Of Geology and Geognosy we know enough: what with the labours of our Werners and Huttons, what with the ardent genius of their disciples, it has come about that now, to many a Royal Society, the Creation of a World is little more mysterious than the cooking of a dumpling;

8

concerning which last, indeed, there have been minds to whom the question, *How the apples were got in,* presented difficulties. Why mention our disquisitions on the Social Contract, on the Standard of Taste, on the Migrations of the Herring? Then, have we not a Doctrine of Rent, a Theory of Value; Philosophies of Language, of History, of Pottery, of Apparitions, of Intoxicating Liquors? Man's whole life and environment have been laid open & elucidated; scarcely a fragment or fibre of his Soul, Body, & Possessions, but has been probed, dissected, distilled, desiccated, & scientifically decomposed: our spiritual Faculties, of which it appears there are not a few, have their Stewarts, Cousins, Royer Collards: every cellular, vascular, muscular Tissue glories in its Lawrences, Majendies, Bichâts. ❡ How, then, comes it, may the reflective mind repeat, that the grand Tissue of all Tissues, the only real Tissue, should have been quite overlooked by Science,—the vestural Tissue, namely, of woollen or other cloth; which Man's Soul wears as its outmost wrappage & overall; wherein his whole other Tissues are included & screened, his whole Faculties work, his whole Self lives, moves, and has its being? For if, now & then, some straggling, broken-winged thinker has cast an owl's-glance into this obscure region, the most have soared over it altogether heedless; regarding Clothes as a property, not an accident, as quite natural and spontaneous, like the leaves of trees, like the plumage of birds. In all

b 9

Preliminary

40 Some Finely Printed Books

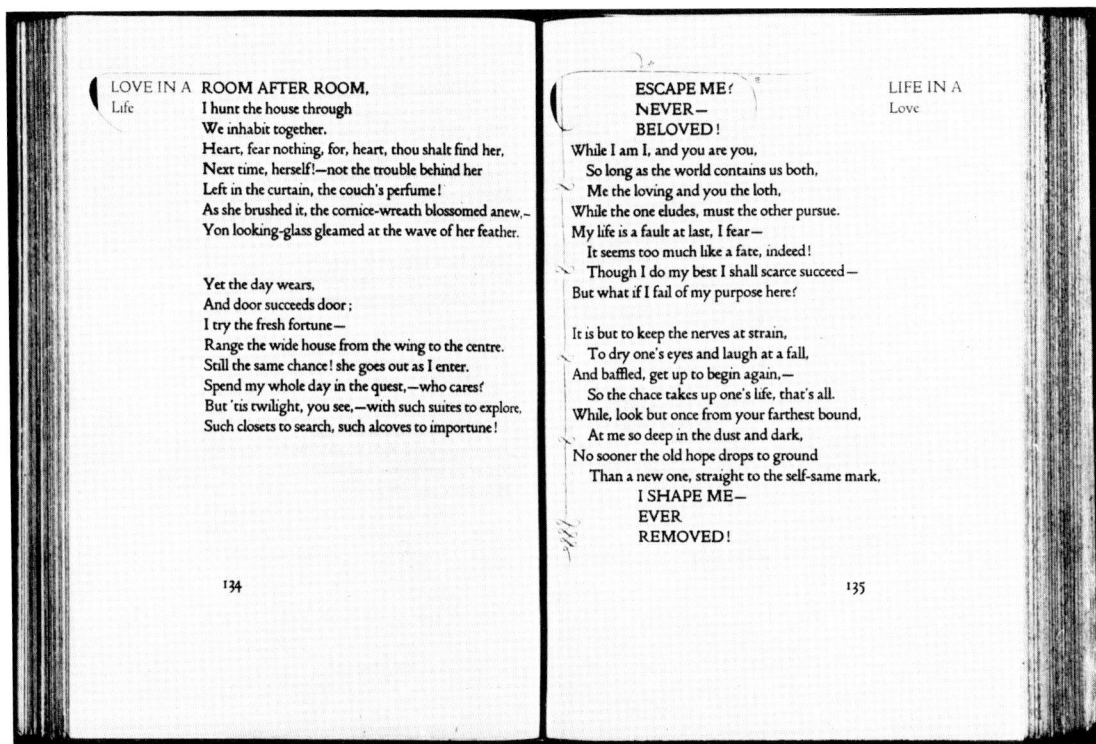

PLATE 21

quently in *Sartor Resartus:* the numerous quotations and book titles requiring underlinings. The Doves type, designed without boldface or italic letters, was not sufficient, and Cobden-Sanderson turned to a commonplace type. Probably a mid-nineteenth-century reinterpretation of a Caslon italic, the light, decorative type is ill at ease next to the darker and more formal Doves. [20]

Edward Johnston (1872–1944), an English calligrapher and neighbor of Cobden-Sanderson, decorated this copy of *Men and Women* after it was printed in 1908. Johnston, the leader of a turn-of-the-century revival of calligraphy who taught Graily Hewitt among several others, also designed many of the Doves initials including those for the Doves *Bible* and *Sartor Resartus*. His invitation to flourish a few copies of *Men and Women* was an afterthought, the delicate tracery fighting for space. Nevertheless, the whimsical designs are colorful, stylistically appropriate, and a welcome relief to the severity of the typography. [21]

21. Robert Browning. *Men and Women.* Hammersmith: Doves Press, 1908. Flourished by Edward Johnston; type design by Emery Walker; book design by T. J. Cobden-Sanderson and Emery Walker. Edition: 250. Two volumes bound as one. 23.9 × 17.2 cm.

Ricketts · The Vale Press

Charles de Sousy Ricketts (1866–1931) was an illustrator, stage-designer, critic, and friend and advisor to several prominent authors and artists of his time. Though modestly successful as a leading practitioner of the diverse styles of English *art nouveau*, Ricketts lived on the edge of poverty for much of his life, exchanging other material comforts in order to build a collection of art. His collection included Greek and Egyptian antiquities, old master drawings and engravings, and Japanese prints—all arranged in rooms lined with wall coverings designed by William Morris—which both fed and reflected Ricketts's eclectic style.

His first book, a *Daphnis and Chloe* printed in 1893, combined a borrowed type with Ricketts's illustrations and initials. The layout of the opening contains a slight variation on Morris's standard approach. The page numbers are moved to the lower left corners of the type blocks to make room for the first word of the following page, called a catchword. Following European practice from the fifteenth through the eighteenth centuries, the catchword is appended to the lower right corner of the text. Ricketts's construction of the opening into three horizontal bands of type, illustration, and type suggests a classical frieze. However, the illustration has the flavor of the Italian Renaissance, especially in the decorations

22. Longus. *Daphnis and Chloe*. Trans. by George Thornley. London: Charles Ricketts, 1893. Illustrations by Charles Ricketts and Charles Shannon; typefounder, [Miller & Richard, designed by Alexander Phemister?]; book design by Charles Ricketts; printed under Ricketts's supervision by Ballantyne Press. Edition: 210. 29.1 × 22.1 cm.

DAPHNIS HIDETH HIMSELF IN THE BOLE OF AN ANCIENT TREE FROM THE AGGRESSIVE INCURSATIONS OF ARMED METHYMNAEANS

CHLOE FLEETH LIKE A HARE OR A BIRD FROM THE INSOLENT PURSUIT OF CERTAIN ARMED MEN OF METHYMNE

to kisse and embrace one another with a bold, impatient fury, which before they never did. Yet of that third remedy which the old Philetas taught, they durst not make experiment; for that was not only an enterprise too bold for Maids, but too high for young Goatherds. Therefore still, as before, they spent their nights without sleep, and with remembrance of what was done, and with complaint of what was not. We have kist one another, and are never the better; we have clipt and embrac't, and that's as good as nothing too. Therefore to lye together naked is the onely remaining remedy of Love. That must be tryed by all means; ther's something in it, without doubt, more efficacious than in a kisse.

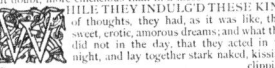HILE THEY INDULG'D THESE KIND of thoughts, they had, as it was like, their sweet, erotic, amorous dreams; and what they did not in the day, that they acted in the night, and lay together stark naked, kissing, clipping,

32

clipping, twining limbs. But the next day, as if they had bin inspired with some stronger Numen, they rose up, and drove their flocks with a kind of violence to the fields, hasting to their kisses again; and, when they saw one another, smiling sweetly ran together. Kisses past, Embraces past, but that third Remedy was wanting; for Daphnis durst not mention it, and Chloe too would not begin; till at length, even by chance, they made this essay of it. They sate both close together upon the trunck of an old Oak and having tasted the sweetness of kisses, they were ingulf'd insatiably in pleasure, and there arose a mutual contention and striving with their clasping arms which made a close compression of their lips; and, when Daphnis hugg'd her to him with a more violent desire, it came about that Chloe inclin'd a little on her side, and Daphnis, following his kisse, fell o'th top on her. And, remembering that they had an image of this in their dreams the night before, they lay a long while clinging

33

together.

PLATE 22

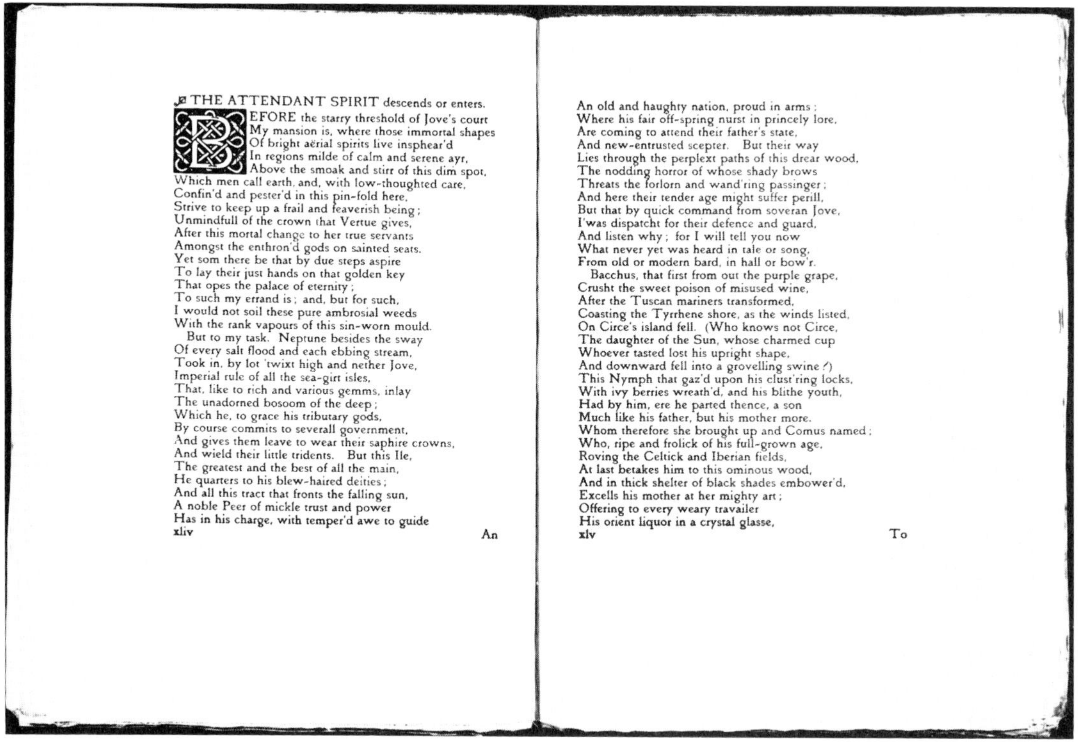

♩ THE ATTENDANT SPIRIT descends or enters.

EFORE the starry threshold of Jove's court
My mansion is, where those immortal shapes
Of bright aërial spirits live insphear'd
In regions milde of calm and serene ayr,
Above the smoak and stirr of this dim spot,
Which men call earth, and, with low-thoughted care,
Confin'd and pester'd in this pin-fold here,
Strive to keep up a frail and feaverish being;
Unmindfull of the crown that Vertue gives,
After this mortal change to her true servants
Amongst the enthron'd gods on sainted seats.
Yet som there be that by due steps aspire
To lay their just hands on that golden key
That opes the palace of eternity;
To such my errand is; and, but for such,
I would not soil these pure ambrosial weeds
With the rank vapours of this sin-worn mould.
  But to my task. Neptune besides the sway
Of every salt flood and each ebbing stream,
Took in, by lot 'twixt high and nether Jove,
Imperial rule of all the sea-girt isles,
That, like to rich and various gemms, inlay
The unadorned bosoom of the deep;
Which he, to grace his tributary gods,
By course commits to severall government,
And gives them leave to wear their saphire crowns,
And wield their little tridents. But this Ile,
The greatest and the best of all the main,
He quarters to his blew-haired deities;
And all this tract that fronts the falling sun,
A noble Peer of mickle trust and power
Has in his charge, with temper'd awe to guide
xliv   An

An old and haughty nation, proud in arms;
Where his fair off-spring nurst in princely lore,
Are coming to attend their father's state,
And new-entrusted scepter. But their way
Lies through the perplext paths of this drear wood,
The nodding horror of whose shady brows
Threats the forlorn and wand'ring passinger;
And here their tender age might suffer perill,
But that by quick command from soveran Jove,
I was dispatcht for their defence and guard,
And listen why; for I will tell you now
What never yet was heard in tale or song,
From old or modern bard, in hall or bow'r.
  Bacchus, that first from out the purple grape,
Crusht the sweet poison of misused wine,
After the Tuscan mariners transformed,
Coasting the Tyrrhene shore, as the winds listed,
On Circe's island fell. (Who knows not Circe,
The daughter of the Sun, whose charmed cup
Whoever tasted lost his upright shape,
And downward fell into a grovelling swine?)
This Nymph that gaz'd upon his clust'ring locks,
With ivy berries wreath'd, and his blithe youth,
Had by him, ere he parted thence, a son
Much like his father, but his mother more.
Whom therefore she brought up and Comus named;
Who, ripe and frolick of his full-grown age,
Roving the Celtick and Iberian fields,
At last betakes him to this ominous wood,
And in thick shelter of black shades embower'd,
Excells his mother at her mighty art;
Offering to every weary travailer
His orient liquor in a crystal glasse,
xlv   To

PLATE 23

of the saddles, bridles, and horsemen's armor as well as the shallow background flattened with patches of diagonal hatching. The only weakness is the uneven printing of the book in which lightly inked pages are found opposite heavily inked counterparts, troubling otherwise beautifully conceived openings. [22]

In 1896 Ricketts printed *The Early Poems of John Milton*, the first book issued under his Vale imprint and the first to be set in Vale type. Although designed without close reference to any other, the Vale face closely resembles Morris's Golden type. A few differences lay in the enlarged enclosures of the lowercase a's and e's, and flattened tail of the lowercase g. The setting widens the spacing between words as well as lines, and Ricketts generally tries to get along without running titles, particularly when setting poetry. Unfortunately he continued the use of the catchword, here detached and drifting away from the text. [23]

23. John Milton. *The Early Poems.* Ed. by Charles Sturt. London: Hacon and Ricketts, [1896.] Illustration, initials, ornaments, type, and book design by Charles Ricketts; printed for Vale Press under Ricketts's supervision by Ballantyne Press. Edition: 310. 27 × 20.6 cm.

24. Percy Bysshe Shelley. *Lyrical Poems.* London: Hacon and Ricketts, 1898. Initial, ornaments, type, and book design by Charles Ricketts; printed for Vale Press under Ricketts's supervision by Ballantyne Press. Edition: 210. 15.2 × 12.1 cm.

25. John Keats. *The Poems.* London: Hacon and Ricketts, 1898. Initials, ornaments, type, and book design by Charles Ricketts; printed for Vale Press under Ricketts's supervision by Ballantyne Press. Edition: 217. 23.9 × 15.4 cm.

CONTENTS.

From the forests & highlands	3
Rarely, rarely, comest thou	6
One word is too often profaned	9
I arise from dreams of thee	10
The flower that smiles to-day	12
That time is dead for ever, child	13
When the lamp is shattered	14
A widow bird sate mourning for her love	16
Oh, world! oh, life! oh, time!	17
Unfathomable Sea!	18
Rough wind, that moanest loud	19
Swiftly walk over the western wave	20
Music, when soft voices die	22
Hail to thee, blithe spirit!	23
Arethusa arose	30
O, wild West Wind	35
I bring fresh showers	40
Life of Life! thy lips enkindle	45
The pale stars are gone!	49
The young moon has fed	51

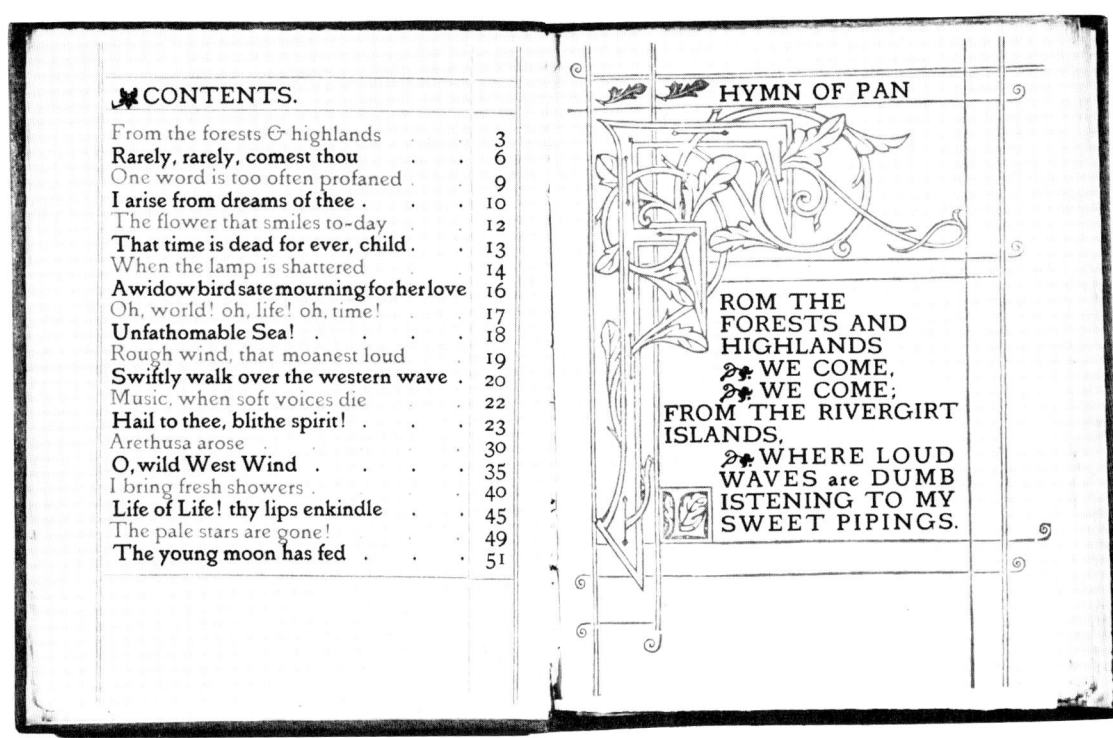

PLATE 24

PLATE 25

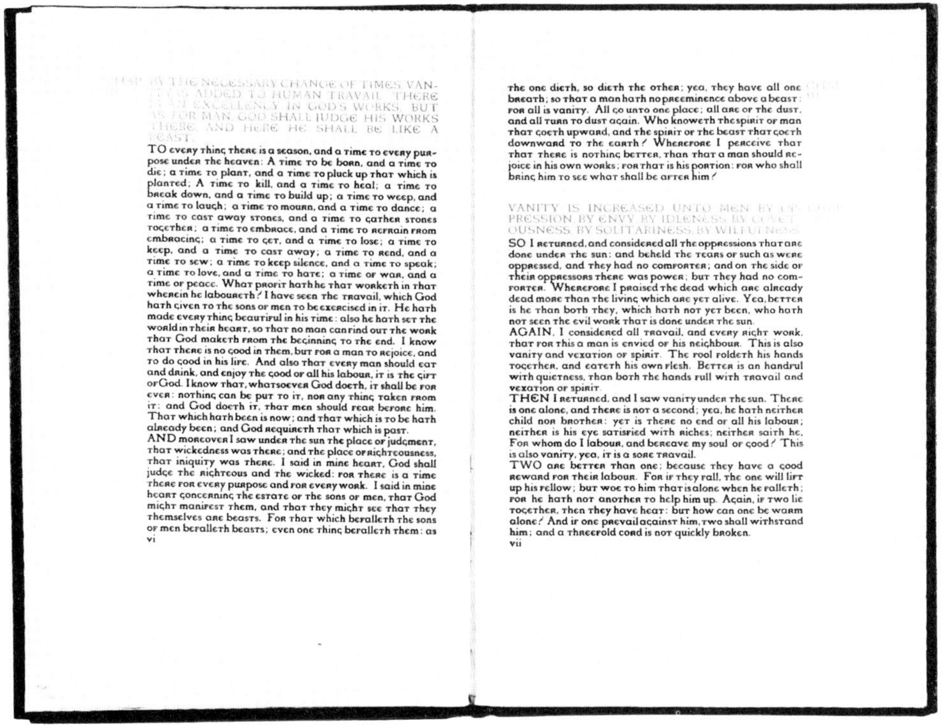

PLATE 26

Ricketts's greatest strength was as a designer of *art nouveau* ornaments. Based on a long, sinuous line, the rippling patterns of his foliate designs often decorated the title pages of his books, as shown here in two works, the *Lyrical Poems of Shelley* and *The Poems of John Keats*, both done in 1898. The silvery tone of his ornaments balances that of the uppercase typography in both books; but the alternating red and black elements on both sides of the opening in the Shelley compete for attention with Ricketts's carefully plotted composition of ruled lines, initials, and type. In the Keats the texture is exquisite, particularly on the left-hand side where the various components merge into a fresh growth of decoration and typography. [24, 25]

The King's type was Ricketts's most original contribution as a type designer. For the type, shown here in its first application in the Vale *Ecclesiastes* (1902), Ricketts grafted certain features of the uncial script, which evolved between the fourth and eighth centuries, onto the basic roman letter form, retaining the serifs. Although Ricketts created upper- and lowercase fonts, the early medieval model only contained one case which mixed the letter forms now distinguished into the two cases. Accordingly, Ricketts designed uppercase forms of the F, G, R, and T as well as the distinctive hump-backed E for the lowercase font. The type compresses easily, yielding a pleasant, grainy texture, interrupted for the reader only by the unfamiliar innovations such as the E and ruptured lowercase g. Ricketts's exotic achievement may well have been the first attempt to translate the uncial form into a text type. [26]

26. *Ecclesiastes; or, The Preacher* and *The Song of Solomon.* London: Hacon and Ricketts, 1902. Type and book design by Charles Ricketts; printed for Vale Press under Ricketts's supervision by Ballantyne Press. Edition: 300. 30.1 × 20.6 cm.

Pissarro · The Eragny Press

With the support of Charles Ricketts, Lucien Pissarro turned his skill as an artist to creating books illustrated with the palette and soft focus of an impressionist, as well as books of early music printed in a sixteenth-century style.

Lucien Pissarro (1863–1944) was the eldest son of the French impressionist painter Camille Pissarro and, having expressed a youthful interest in painting, was taught by his father and friends of his father, notably Manet and Cézanne. But early on Pissarro began to specialize in color printing, and by 1890, believing that the French were unreceptive toward fine graphic art, he left for England. In London he was introduced to Charles Ricketts, who appreciated Pissarro's gift. Ricketts helped arrange the publication of Pissarro's first book, and allowed him to use the Vale type for several subsequent publications of Pissarro's Eragny Press, named for his home village in Normandy.

His first book, an *art nouveau*-cum-impressionist *Queen of the Fishes*, was finished in 1894. Like Pine's *Horace*, the text is printed not from movable type, but from a single block per page. In this case, however, the blocks were reproduced photomechanically from Pissarro's limpid handwritten manuscript. Although the uneven inking of the type and monochromatic illustrations is due to Pissarro's inexperience as a printer, the light tone of his ink was deliberate. His plan was to reduce the contrasts of ink and paper to a subtle impres-

27. Margaret Rust. *The Queen of the Fishes*. London: "Vale Publications," 1894. Illustrations, ornaments, script, and book design by Lucien Pissarro; printed by Eragny Press. No. 56 of 150. 19.4 × 13.6 cm.

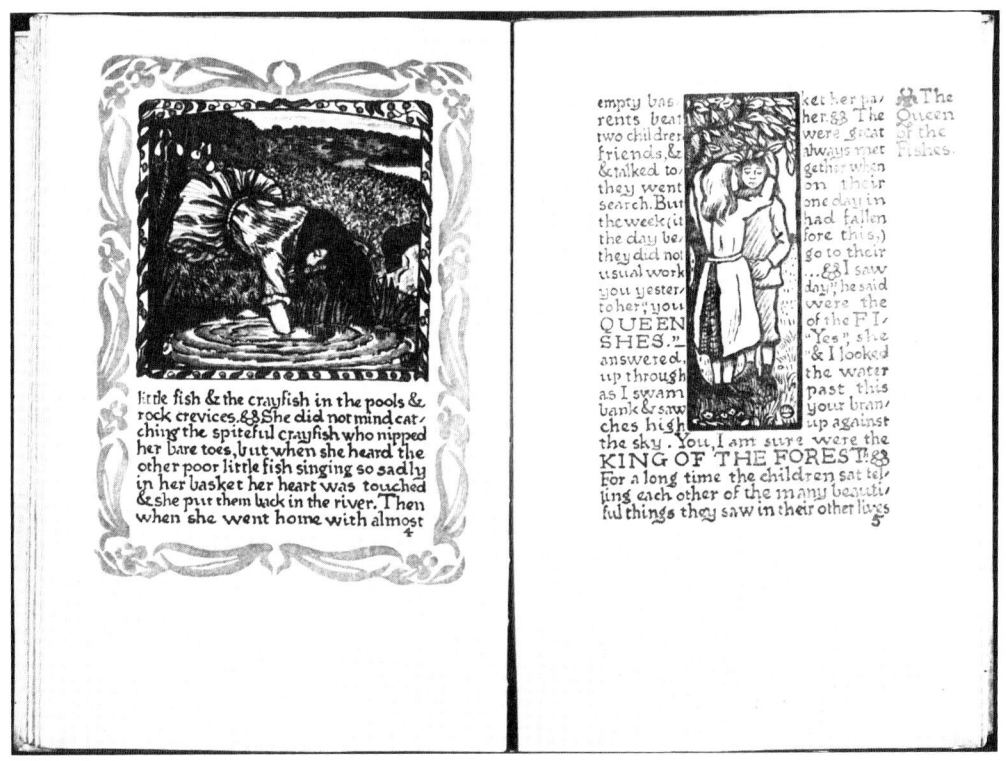

PLATE 27

sionist interplay of pastel hues. Pissarro's skill as a craftsman found its greatest expression in his color illustrations such as the one on the left. Five wood engravings, one for each hue, were required to build up the mellow coloring and hazy atmosphere out of overlays of pointillistic stipplings and faint hatching. [27]

The Brook type, designed by Pissarro to replace the Vale type which Ricketts withdrew from use in 1903 and later destroyed, is shown here in the Eragny *Areopagitica*, printed in 1904. The type, as one might expect, is very close to Ricketts's Vale, the only major differences—such as the flapping tail of the lowercase g—carried over from Pissarro's script. A subtle variation which sets the Brook type apart from most of the others of the same period is the irregularity of the individual letter forms. The result is a less precise, almost hand-penned appearance. The initials are left over from Pissarro's work with the Vale type, however, and since Brook type is slightly smaller, when it is set with normal spacing between lines it does not quite match the height of the initials, leaving narrow gaps below each block. The naive charm of the initials derives from the rough-hewn quality of the engraving and lack of regard for the relationships of letter, foliage, and frame, a refreshing departure from the tightly organized initials of Morris and Ricketts. [28]

Applying his expertise in printing with color, Pissarro designed two books of early music: *Some Old French and English Ballads* and *Songs by Ben Jonson*, issued respectively in 1905 and 1906. The method Pissarro followed, based on sixteenth-century practice, called for printing the red

28. John Milton. *Areopagitica*. Hammersmith: Eragny Press, 1904. Initials, ornaments, type, and book design by Lucien Pissarro. Second issue. Edition: 160. 27.5 × 21.7 cm.

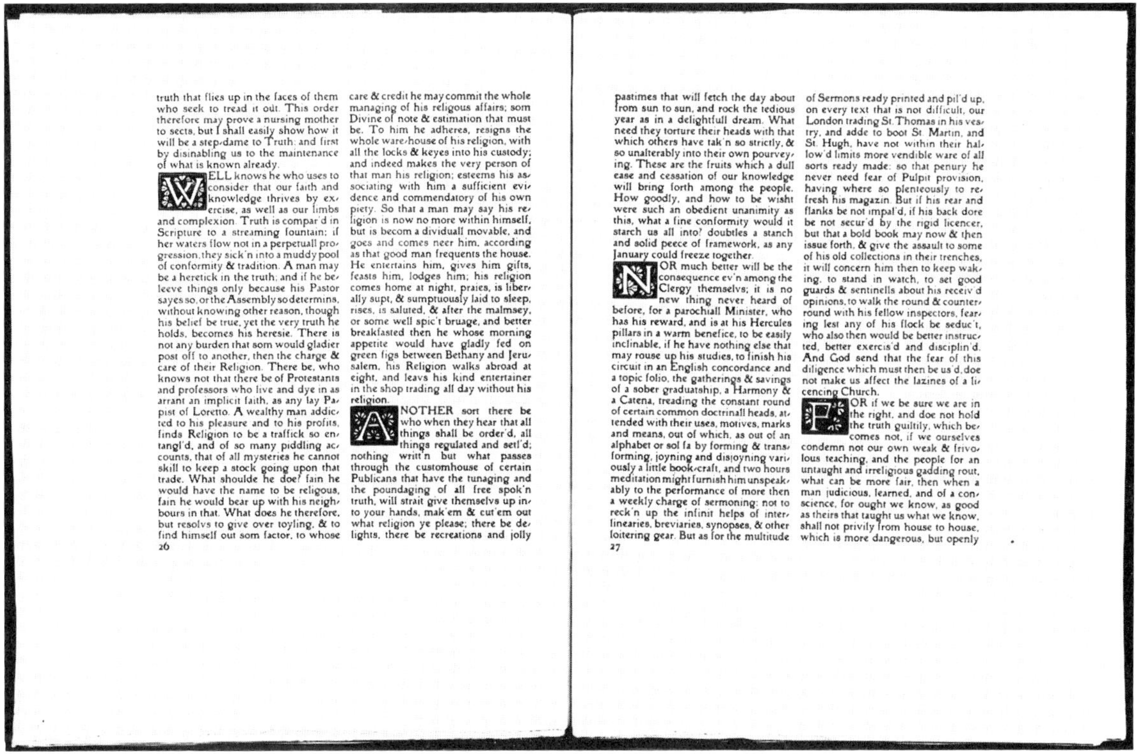

truth that flies up in the faces of them who seek to tread it out. This order therefore may prove a nursing mother to sects, but I shall easily show how it will be a step-dame to Truth: and first by disinabling us to the maintenance of what is known already.

WELL knows he who uses to consider that our faith and knowledge thrives by exercise, as well as our limbs and complexion. Truth is compar'd in Scripture to a streaming fountain; if her waters flow not in a perpetuall progression, they sick'n into a muddy pool of conformity & tradition. A man may be a hereticik in the truth, and if he beleeve things only because his Pastor sayes so, or the Assembly so determins, without knowing other reason, though his belief be true, yet the very truth he holds, becomes his heresie. There is not any burden that som would gladier post off to another, then the charge & care of their Religion. There be, who knows not that there be of Protestants and professors who live and dye in as arrant an implicit faith, as any lay Papist of Loretto. A wealthy man addicted to his pleasure and to his profits, finds Religion to be a traffick so entangl'd, and of so many piddling accounts, that of all mysteries he cannot skill to keep a stock going upon that trade. What shoulde he doe? fain he would have the name to be religous, fain he would bear up with his neighbours in that. What does he therefore, but resolvs to give over toyling, & to find himself out som factor, to whose care & credit he may commit the whole managing of his religious affairs; som Divine of note & estimation that must be. To him he adheres, resigns the whole ware-house of his religion, with all the locks & keyes into his custody; and indeed makes the very person of that man his religion; esteems his associating with him a sufficient evidence and commendatory of his own piety. So that a man may say his religion is now no more within himself, but is becom a dividuall movable, and goes and comes neer him, according as that good man frequents the house. He entertains him, gives him gifts, feasts him, lodges him, his religion comes home at night, praies, is liberally supt, & sumptuously laid to sleep, rises, is saluted, & after the malmsey, or some well spic't bruage, and better breakfasted then he whose morning appetite would have gladly fed on green figs between Bethany and Jerusalem, his Religion walks abroad at eight, and leavs his kind entertainer in the shop trading all day without his religion.

ANOTHER sort there be who when they hear that all things shall be order'd, all things regulated and settl'd; nothing writt'n but what passes through the customhouse of certain Publicans that have the tunaging and the poundaging of all free spok'n truth, will strait give themselves up intoto your hands, mak'em & cut'em out what religion ye please; there be delights, there be recreations and jolly

26

paastimes that will fetch the day about from sun to sun, and rock the tedious year as in a delightfull dream. What need they torture their heads with that which others have tak'n so strictly, & so unalterably into their own pourveying. These are the fruits which a dull ease and cesation of our knowledge will bring forth among the people. How goodly, and how to be wisht were such an obedient unanimity as this, what a fine conformity would it starch us all into? doubtles a stanch and solid peece of framework, as any January could freeze together.

FOR much better will be the consequence ev'n among the Clergy themselvs; it is no new thing never heard of before, for a parochiall Minister, who has his reward, and is at his Hercules pillars in a warm benefice, to be easily inclinable, if he have nothing else that may rouse up his studies, to finish his circuit in an English concordance and a topic folio, the gatherings & savings of a sober graduatship, a Harmony & a Catena, treading the constant round of certain common doctrinall heads, attended with their uses, motives, marks and means, out of which, as out of an alphabet or sol fa by forming & transforming, joyning and disjoyning variously a little book-craft, and two hours meditation might furnish him unspeakably to the performance of more then a weekly charge of sermoning: not to reck'n up the infinit helps of interlinearies, breviaries, synopses, & other loitering gear. But as for the multitude of Sermons ready printed and pil'd up, on every text that is not difficult, our London trading St. Thomas in his veatry, and adde to boot St. Martin, and St. Hugh, have not within their hallow'd limits more vendible ware of all sorts ready made: so that penury he never need fear of Pulpit provision, having where so plenteously to refresh his magazin. But if his rear and flanks be not impal'd, if his back dore be not secur'd by the rigid licencer, but that a bold book may now & then issue forth, & give the assault to some of his old collections in their trenches, it will concern him then to keep waking, to stand in watch, to set good guards & sentinells about his receiv'd opinions, to walk the round & counterround with his fellow inspectors, fearing lest any of his flock be seduc't, who also then would be better instructed, better exercis'd and disciplin'd. And God send the fear of this diligence which must then be us'd, doe not make us affect the lazines of a licencing Church.

FOR if we be sure we are in the right, and doe not hold the truth guiltily, which becomes not, if we ourselves condemn not our own weak & frivolous teaching, and the people for an untaught and irreligious gadding rout, what can be more fair, then when a man judicious, learned, and of a conscience, for ought we know, as good as theirs that taught us what we know, shall not privily from house to house,which is more dangerous, but openly

27

PLATE 28

PLATE 29

staves first and the black notes, key, and measure markings last. He had to be careful to line up or register the sheet of red staves precisely with the black type, otherwise the music would be inaccurate and very likely unperformable. Another difficulty lay in the setting of the black notes. Unlike letter type, which is set in straight lines, music type must be spaced vertically as well as horizontally, requiring special leading and meticulous setting. [29, 30]

Pissarro's unique and most personalized book design after *Queen of the Fishes* was *Album de poëmes tirés*, printed in 1911. The tail ornaments are *art nouveau*, but overall the book—consistent with its subject—is redolent with *japonisme*, the late nineteenth-century French fascination with Oriental decorative arts. Everything, from the tiny lotus-leaf marks to the illustrations, and from the paper to the binding, points toward the Far East. The division of the text with numerous vertical and horizontal rulings, taken from traditional Japanese book design, seems unnecessarily halting. Perhaps Pissarro, always more a part of his father's generation than his own, wanted his public to linger over the dreamy ennui of this work. [31]

29. *Some Old French and English Ballads.* Ed. by Robert Steele. Hammersmith: Eragny Press, 1905. Illustration, initials, ornaments, type, and book design by Lucien Pissarro. Edition: 200. 21.2 × 14 cm.

30. Ben Jonson. *Songs by Ben Jonson.* Hammersmith: Eragny Press, 1906. Frontispiece, initials, ornaments, type, and book design by Lucien Pissarro. Edition: 175. 21.2 × 14 cm.

31. *Album de poëmes tirés du livre de jade.* Trans. and ed. by Judith Gautier. Hammersmith: Eragny Press, 1911. Illustrations, initials, ornaments, type, and book design by Lucien Pissarro. No. 108 of 130. 19.6 × 13.3 cm.

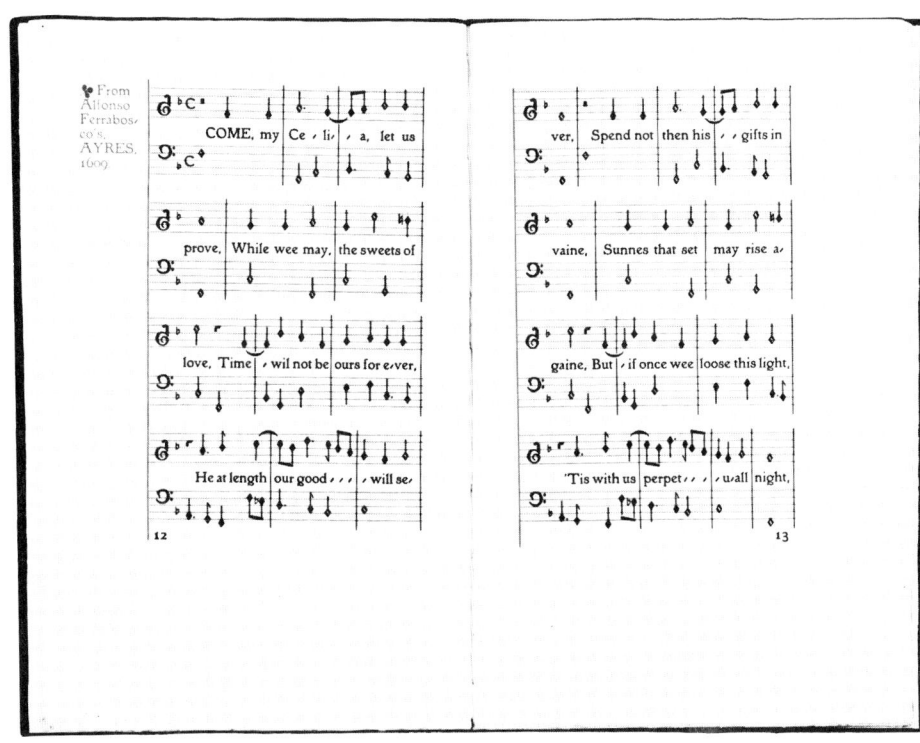

PLATE 30

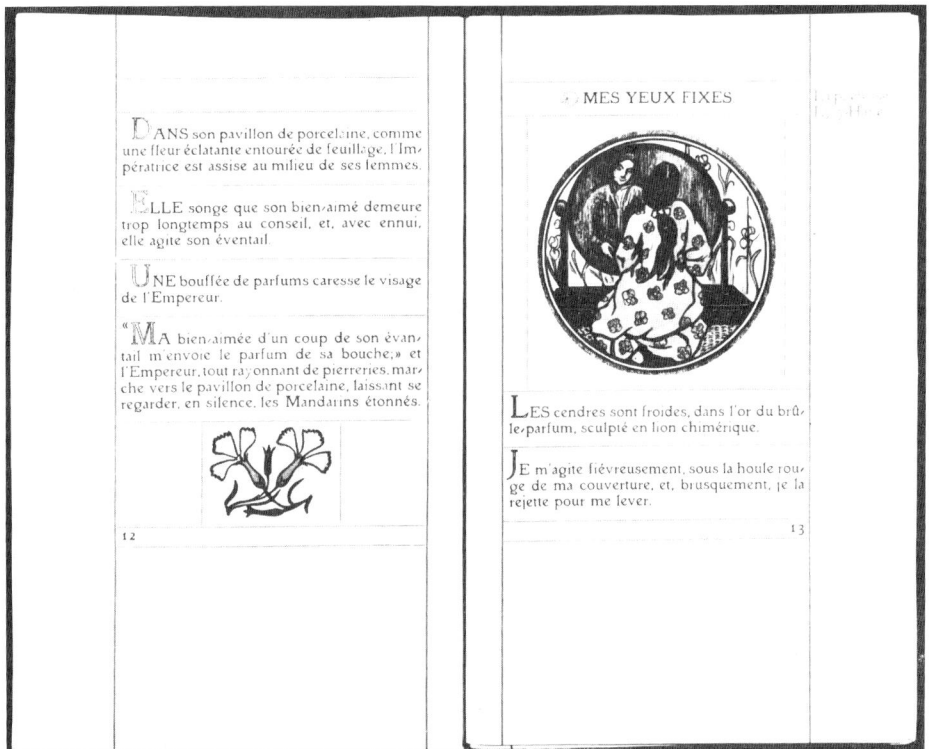

PLATE 31

Updike · The Merrymount Press

Daniel Berkeley Updike, among the first Americans to assimilate Morris's work, evolved a personal style based on principles of simplicity and clarity.

Updike (1860–1941) was brought up in a New England home with "a deepened religious sense" rooted in a firm Episcopalian background, an affiliation he maintained throughout his private and professional life. Without prior experience, he found a job in the printing trade as an errand boy for the Boston publisher, Houghton, Mifflin & Company. Possessing an intuitive skill in design, Updike moved up to a position designing promotional layouts, gaining several years of experience before being transferred to the fine book subsidiary to design books. But friction with his superiors and a commission from an Episcopalian friend led Updike to set out on his own, eventually founding his Merrymount Press.

The commission, completed in 1896, was for *The Altar Book,* a production in which Updike's role was more akin to that of an orchestral conductor than that of a book designer. The borders, initials, and type were designed by Bertram Grosvenor Goodhue (1869–1924), a young architect and sometime typographer who later designed Rockefeller Chapel on the University of Chicago campus. The illustrations were designed by Robert Anning Bell

32. *The Altar Book.* According to the use of the American Church. Boston: Daniel Berkeley Updike and Harold Brown, 1896. Illustrations by Robert Anning Bell; borders, initials, and type design by Bertram Grosvenor Goodhue; book design by Daniel Berkeley Updike; typeset at Merrymount Press; printed by De Vinne Press. Edition: 350. 38.1 × 28.9 cm.

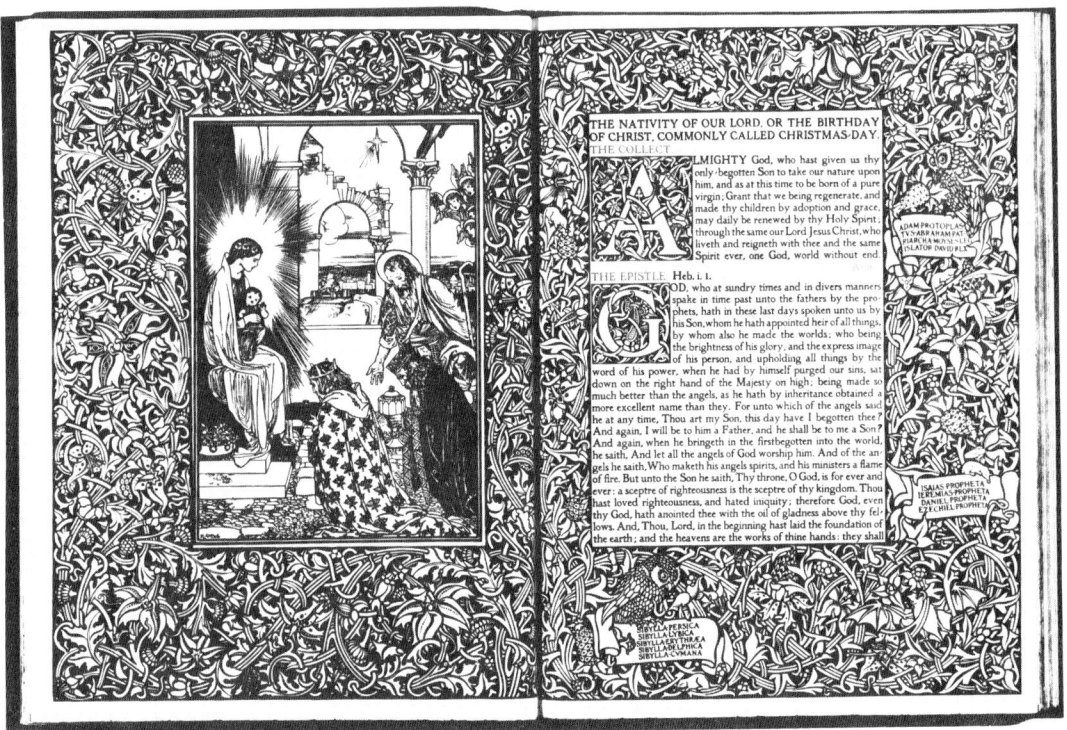

PLATE 32

lium, et lapis onychinus. Et nomen fluvii secundi Gehon; ipse est qui circumit omnem terram Æthiopiæ. Nomen vero fluminis tertii, Tygris; ipse vadit contra Assyrios. Fluvius autem quartus, ipse est Euphrates. Tulit ergo Dominus Deus hominem, et posuit eum in paradiso voluptatis, ut operaretur, et custodiret illum. Præcepitque ei dicens: Ex omni ligno paradisi comede: de ligno autem scientiæ boni et mali ne comedas: in quocumque enim die comederis ex eo, morte morieris. Dixit quoque Dominus Deus: Non est bonum, esse hominem solum: faciamus ei adjutorium simile sibi. Formatis igitur, Dominus Deus, de humo cunctis animantibus terræ, et universis volatilibus cœli, adduxit ea ad Adam, ut videret quid vocaret ea; omne enim quod vocavit Adam animæ viventis, ipsum est nomen ejus. Appellavitque Adam nominibus suis cuncta animantia, et universa volatilia cœli, et omnes bestias terræ; Adæ vero non inveniebatur adjutor similis ejus. Immisit ergo Dominus Deus soporem in Adam; cumque obdormisset, tulit unam de costis ejus, et replevit carnem pro ea. Et ædificavit Dominus Deus costam, quam tulerat de Adam, in mulierem, et adduxit eam ad Adam. Dixitque Adam: Hoc nunc os

bdellium and the onyx stone. And the name of the second river is Gihon: the same is it that compasseth the whole land of Ethiopia. And the name of the third river is Hiddekel: that is it which goeth toward the east of Assyria. And the fourth river is Euphrates. And the Lord God took the man, and put him into the garden of Eden to dress it and to keep it. And the Lord God commanded the man, saying, Of every tree of the garden thou mayest freely eat: but of the tree of the knowledge of good and evil, thou shalt not eat of it: for in the day that thou eatest thereof thou shalt surely die. And the Lord God said, It is not good that the man should be alone; I will make him an help meet for him. And out of the ground the Lord God formed every beast of the field, and every fowl of the air; and brought them unto Adam to see what he would call them: and whatsoever Adam called every living creature, that was the name thereof. And Adam gave names to all cattle, and to the fowl of the air, and to every beast of the field; but for Adam there was not found an help meet for him. And the Lord God caused a deep sleep to fall upon Adam, and he slept: and he took one of his ribs, and closed

PLATE 33

(1863–1933), an Englishman; and the printing was carried out under the supervision of Theodore De Vinne (1828–1914), a distinguished New York printer. Yet Updike succeeded in directing his forces to create a work which closely approximates the look and unity of a Kelmscott Press book. Updike felt that Goodhue's type, though based directly on Jenson, was "seduced by Morris's unduly black" interpretation and "merely modified the heaviness of the Morris fonts." But the type was designed to work on large pages and when viewed at a slight distance, as though placed on a lectern, the type blends into a pleasant pattern without sacrificing legibility. Goodhue's borders, however, are too irregular and coarse to blend into the same typographic texture as the illustration and type. Part of the reason for this is Goodhue's reluctance to abstract his highly naturalistic flora and fauna into finer and more regular, if less realistic, patterns. [32]

Updike's familiarity with the Kelmscott style was exercised again in a publication of illustrations created for an edition by Morris which was never completed. The artist was Edward Burne-Jones (1833–1898), a painter, illustrator, and life-long friend of Morris. Burne-Jones, who designed illustrations for a number of Kelmscott books, began drawings for a project which was ended by Morris's death. Subsequent to Burne-Jones's death the drawings were transferred to wood so that they could be published in a book that would display the images as they were originally meant to be viewed. The result, *In the Dawn of the World* printed in 1903, captures the essential

33. *In the Dawn of the World.* Boston: Charles E. Goodspeed, 1903. Illustrations by Edward Burne-Jones, engraved after latter's death by Robert Catterson-Smith; type design by Bertram Grosvenor Goodhue; book design by Daniel Berkeley Updike; printed by Merrymount Press. No. 76 of 185. 35.4 × 22.3 cm.

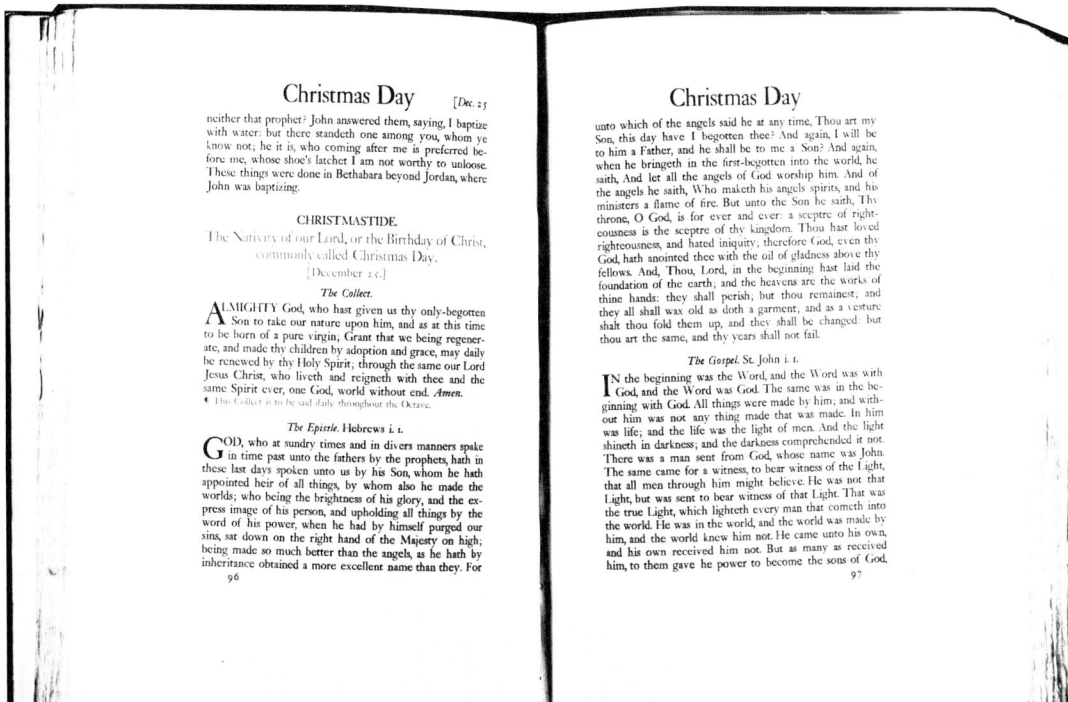

PLATE 34

texture and proportions of a Kelmscott book without diverting attention from the illustrations. Updike, setting the text in Goodhue's type, wisely avoided Morris's frills, such as the Gothic ornaments, initials, and paragraph marks. The text is merely shaped to provide pedestals upon which the illustrations have been mounted. [33]

The Book of Common Prayer, finished in 1930, is the fullest expression of Updike's personal style. Four presses were asked to submit specimen sheets in a competition which Updike won due largely to his knowledge of the Episcopal faith and the "liturgical requirements and practical use of the Prayer Book." The beauty of the book comes from its simplicity. Set close in Janson, a type that originated in the late seventeenth century, the page layouts derive their strength from Morris's proportions of text to paper, distribution of margins, and page number placements. But Updike has stripped the text bare by eliminating all ornaments, relying on enlarged Janson initials, Janson italic, and a sparing use of rubrication, to decorate the book. The book is as American as a piece of colonial furniture, austere and solemn without being plain. [34]

34. *The Book of Common Prayer.* According to the use of the Protestant Episcopal Church in the United States of America. Boston: Joint Commission on the Revision and Enrichment of the Book of Common Prayer, 1930. Typefounder, [Nicholas Kis] Stempel, "Janson"; book design by Daniel Berkeley Updike; printed by Merrymount Press. Edition: 500. 35.5 × 25.5 cm.

Goudy · The Village Press

Frederic W. Goudy refined his skills as a type and book designer through a number of personally printed books which reflect the lessons of Morris and his English successors.

One of this nation's most productive and inventive type designers, Goudy (1865–1947) spent his early years moving from job to job before arriving in Chicago by 1895 where he found work as a bookkeeper in a secondhand bookstore. A fascination with graphic design and processes led him into an abortive commercial printing venture, exposure to Vale and Kelmscott presswork, and subsequent experiments in typographic design. By the turn of the century Goudy began to receive a trickle of regular assignments as a free-lance designer, and in 1902, a request from a Chicago firm for an advertising typeface. The design Goudy submitted, though approved in principle, was too costly for his client's purposes. Left with the design and armed with outside support, Goudy had the design cast and used it as the first font for another printing venture, the Village Press.

The first Village Press book, *Printing*, was completed in 1903. It is set in Goudy's Village type based "more or less on the types of Jenson as exhibited in Morris's Golden type, in the Doves . . . Merrymount, and types of that ilk." The Village type approximates the calligraphic spirit of Jenson more closely than its predecessors,

35. William Morris and Emery Walker. *Printing*. Reprinted from *Arts and Crafts Essays by Members of the Arts and Crafts Exhibition Society*, 1893. Park Ridge, Illinois: Village Press, 1903. Initial, ornaments, type, and book design by Frederic W. Goudy. No. 57 of 231. 23.6 × 18.2 cm.

12 to be comfortable reading: the size known as "Long primer" ought to be the smallest size used in a book meant to be read. Here, again, if the practice of "leading" were retrenched larger type could be used without enhancing the price of a book. ❧One very important matter in "setting up" for fine printing is the "spacing," that is, the lateral distance of words from one another. In good printing the spaces between the words should be as near as possible equal (it is impossible that they should be quite equal except in lines of poetry); modern printers understand this, but it is only practised in the very best establishments. But another point which they should attend to they almost always disregard; this is the tendency to the formation of ugly meandering white lines or "rivers" in the page, a blemish which can be nearly, though not wholly, avoided by care and forethought, the desirable thing being "the breaking of the line" as in bonding masonry or brickwork, thus:≡≡≡≡ The general solidity of a page is much to be sought for: modern printers generally overdo the "whites" in the spacing, a defect probably forced on them by the characterless quality of the letters. For where these are boldly and carefully designed, and each letter is thoroughly individual in form, the words may be set much closer together, without loss of clearness. No definite rules, however, except the avoidance of "rivers" and excess of white, can be given for the spacing, which

requires the constant exercise of judgment and taste on 13 the part of the printer. ❧The position of the page on the paper should be considered if the book is to have a satisfactory look. Here once more the almost invariable modern practice is in opposition to a natural sense of proportion. From the time when books first took their present shape till the end of the sixteenth century, or indeed later, the page so lay on the paper that there was more space allowed to the bottom and fore margin than to the top and back of the paper, thus:

the unit of the book being looked on as the two pages forming an opening. The modern printer, in the teeth

PLATE 35

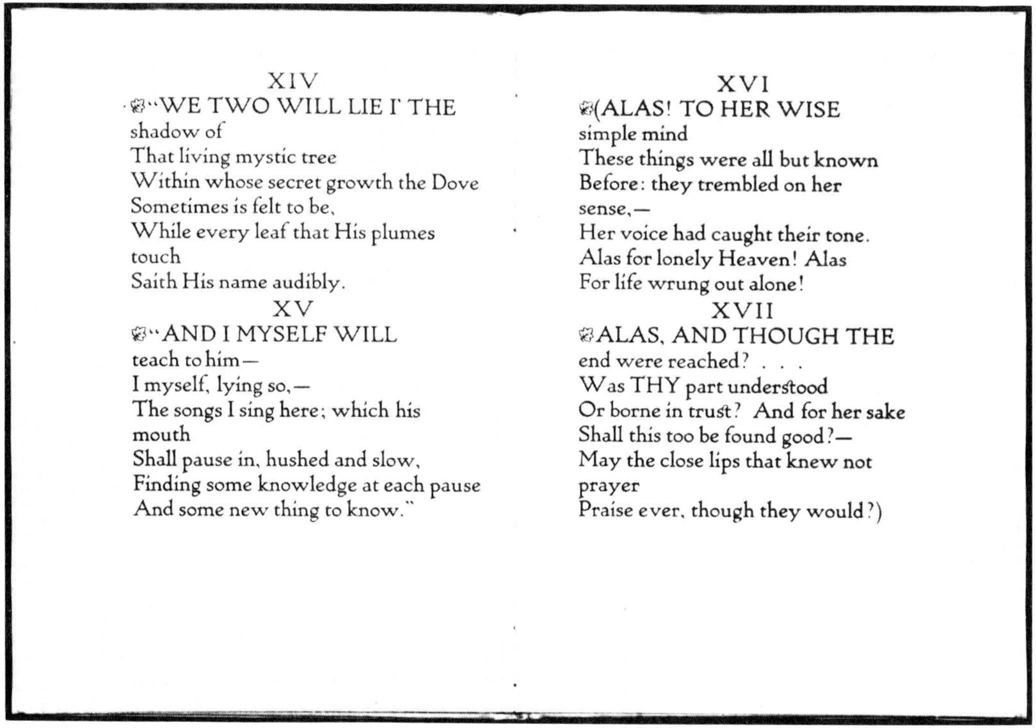

XIV

"WE TWO WILL LIE I' THE
shadow of
That living mystic tree
Within whose secret growth the Dove
Sometimes is felt to be,
While every leaf that His plumes touch
Saith His name audibly.

XV

"AND I MYSELF WILL
teach to him—
I myself, lying so,—
The songs I sing here; which his mouth
Shall pause in, hushed and slow,
Finding some knowledge at each pause
And some new thing to know."

XVI

(ALAS! TO HER WISE
simple mind
These things were all but known
Before: they trembled on her sense,—
Her voice had caught their tone.
Alas for lonely Heaven! Alas
For life wrung out alone!

XVII

ALAS, AND THOUGH THE
end were reached? . . .
Was THY part understood
Or borne in trust? And for her sake
Shall this too be found good?—
May the close lips that knew not prayer
Praise ever, though they would?)

PLATE 36

particularly in the stems, which swell as they ascend or descend toward the wedge-shaped serifs, and the slightly irregular tilt of the swaying lowercase letters. Goudy's most noticeable variations are the wing-shaped dots over the i's and the pointed, triangular shape of the bowl on the lowercase g. The pages of this essay by Morris and Walker are set with a clear understanding and self-conscious reverence for the work of the two, down to the details of the woodcut illustrations designed to illustrate the authors' points. [35]

However, Goudy's skill was not limited to type and book design. He could also create light, unobtrusive leaf ornaments to be used as paragraph marks, and fine borders and initials, as shown in his editions of *The Blessed Damozel* and *A Dissertation Upon Roast Pig*, printed respectively in 1903 and 1904. The right-hand border for *Dissertation* (the left side a mirror-image reproduction of the right) is an intricate and delicately rendered pattern that frames but does not overwhelm the typography. The woodcut title block, an enlargement of the type, is weakened by the uncertain spacing particularly noticeable in the distribution of the letters for "UPON." Goudy designed the unusual initial M in which the black mass is softened with a carefully tailored white outline, and decorated with foliage that

36. Dante Gabriel Rossetti. *The Blessed Damozel.* Reprinted from *The Germ.* No. 2. Feb., 1850. Park Ridge, Illinois: Village Press, 1903. Initial, ornaments, type, and book design by Frederic W. Goudy. Edition: 110. 16.1 × 12 cm.

37. Charles Lamb. *A Dissertation Upon Roast Pig.* Park Ridge, Illinois: Village Press, 1904. Initials, ornaments, type, and book design by Frederic W. Goudy. Edition: 215. 16.3 × 12 cm.

38. Robert Browning. *Rabbi Ben Ezra.* Hingham, Massachusetts: Village Press, 1904. Illustration and ornaments by W. A. Dwiggins; type and book design by Frederic W. Goudy. No. 130 of 173. 20.5 × 13.2 cm.

PLATE 37

PLATE 38

heuy and sorouful, and he tolde to his norice hym thought ther cam a named Wolwelyne. And fayr byrd whiche flewgh whan he had tolde to her up to heuen wyth grete alle hys dreme, she was joye. And anon after thys ful heuy, & tolde to hym

dreme he awoke, & was what hit mente, and sayd alle abasshid of thys his suster and the trayter dreme, whiche anon after Askaberde had falsely

conspired his deth. For she said to hym, that he had promysed to Quendrede to slee the, and that signefyeth that he smytheth doun the tree that stode by thy beddes syde. And the byrd that thou sawest flee up to heuen signefyeth thy soule that angellys shal bere up to heuen after thy martydom. And anon after thys Askaberde desired the kyng that he shold goo and disporte hym by the wodes side named Clent, & as he walkid the kyng was al heuy & leyd hym doun to slepe, and thenne this fals traytour purposed to haue slayn the kyng, and began to make the pyt to bury hym in.

BUT anon as God wold the kyng awoke, & sayd to thys askaberd that he laboured in vayn, ffor God wyl not that I dye in thys place. But take thys smalle rodde, and there as thou shalt sette it in the erthe, ther shal I be martred. & thenne they went forth to gydre a good way thens, tyl they cam to an hawthorn, and there he pyght the rodde in therthe, and forthwith incontynent it bare grene leuys, & sodenly it wexe to a grete asshe tree, the whiche stondeth there yet unto thys day, & is called Kenelms asshe, & there this Askaberd smote of

PLATE 39

helps define the space surrounding the initial without filling it. [36, 37]

For the frontispiece and title page of his edition of *Rabbi Ben Ezra*, printed in 1904, Goudy turned to his young protegé William A. Dwiggins. Recalling this collaboration, Dwiggins (1880–1956), who later became a distinguished illustrator, type, and book designer in his own right, wrote: "I think the picture was my third attempt to make a woodcut. It was . . . cut with a knife on the side of a plank, in the Oriental way, through a drawing pasted down on the wood." Dwiggins's raw talent brought to the illustration an elemental power that shows in its unqualified rendering and direct emotional appeal. Goudy's setting balances the illustration with the title page, and his red inking of the vine softens the steely ornament. [38]

Goudy, like St. John Hornby, toyed early on with a black letter type. Similar to the Ashendene experiment with an old English black letter face, Goudy's *The Lyf of Seynt Kenelme* was printed just four years later in 1905. The initials were inked separately using a special technique whereby several colors are only partially blended to arrive at the "rainbow" effect shown here. [39]

39. *The Lyf of Seynt Kenelme*. Reprinted from William Caxton's *Golden Legend*. Hingham, Massachusetts: Village Press, 1905. Illustrations taken from *The Quest*, 1894–1896; typefounder, American Type Founders, "Flemish"; initials and book design by Frederic W. Goudy. Edition: 160. 16.9 × 13.1 cm.

Wiegand · The Bremer-Presse

Under the guidance of Willi Wiegand, the Bremer-Presse concentrated on creating handsome editions based solely on typefaces designed with machine precision and calligraphic introductory words and initials.

Established in 1911 by a group of German artisans and intellectuals, the Bremer-Presse found administrative and aesthetic direction in Wiegand (1884–1961), the highly educated son of a German industrialist. Wiegand was an energetic manager with the sharp eye and sensitive hand of a meticulous craftsman. He designed all four of the Bremer-Presse house types, and was instrumental in creating the distinctive quality of its most notable books.

La divina commedia, printed in 1921, is set in Wiegand's Antiqua. Like the Ashendene Subiaco, this type was designed with reference to two fifteenth-century models, a Gothic and a Venetian roman. Characteristics of both can be found in the weight and calligraphic tapering of the stems and serifs, and the angular bowls and crowns of the lowercase font. Particularly distinguishing features of Wiegand's design are the foot serifs, which point to the right only, and his variants, differentiated by width, of the lowercase a, f, i, and t. These variants enabled Wiegand to achieve a closer and more balanced letter spacing. For example, in the setting of the word "tutto" in the second line from the bottom on the left-hand page, Wiegand has set the first t (one

40. Dante Alighieri. *La divina commedia*. Ed. by Berthold Wiese. Munich: Bremer-Presse, 1921. Titles and initials designed by Anna Simons; type and book design by Willi Wiegand. No. 41 of 300. 34.2 × 21.3 cm.

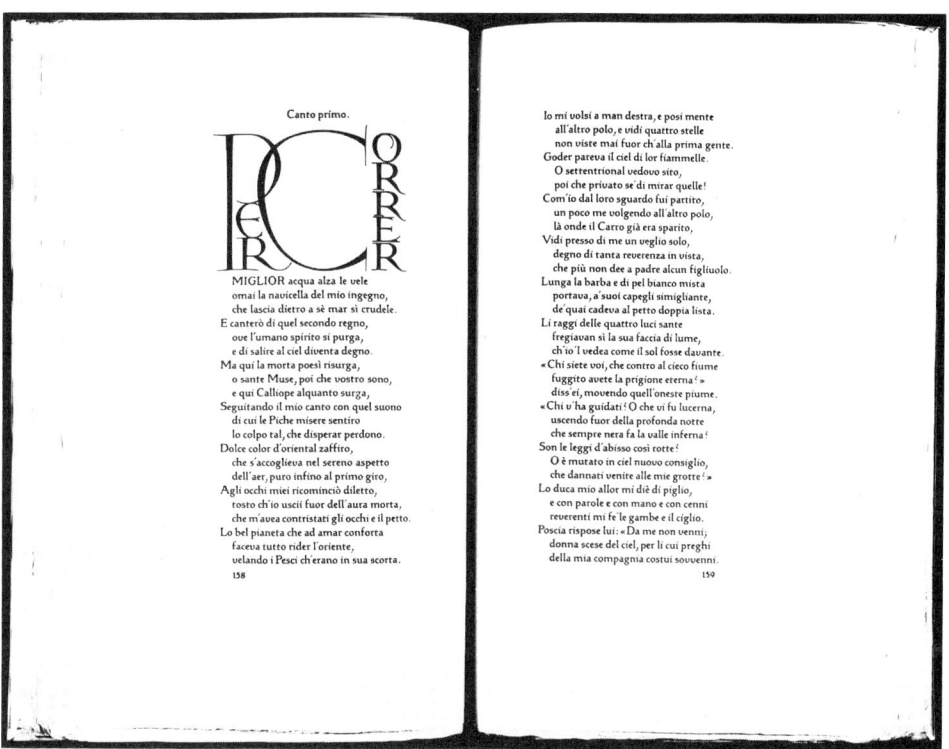

PLATE 40

of three variations based on the length of the horizontal stroke) with the medium-width sized t because of the leftward jutting serif on the u. The other two t's are the long version, the second to hold it an arm's length from the third, and the third to fill the space to the top of the o. [40]

The similarity of the style and placement of the Bremer-Presse initials and introductory words to that of the Ashendene Press is more than coincidental. Anna Simons (1871–1951), the German calligrapher and type designer who fashioned most of the Bremer initials, studied with Edward Johnston as had Ashendene's Graily Hewitt.

41. Anna Simons. *Titel und Initialen für die Bremer-Presse.* Munich: Bremer-Presse, 1926. Printed from original blocks designed by Anna Simons. Edition: 220. 46.5 × 36.5 cm.

42. Homer. ΙΛΙΑΣ. Ed. by Eduard Schwartz. Munich: Bremer-Presse, 1923. Type and book design by Willi Wiegand. No. 538 of 615. 35.9 × 23 cm.

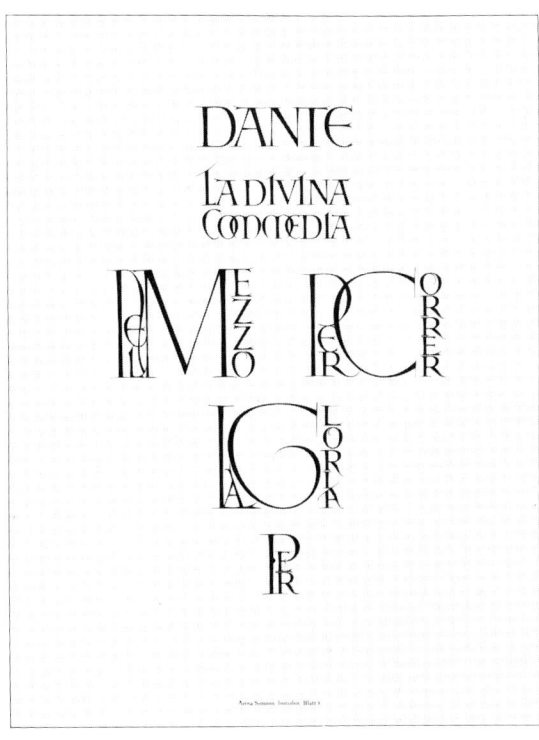

PLATE 41

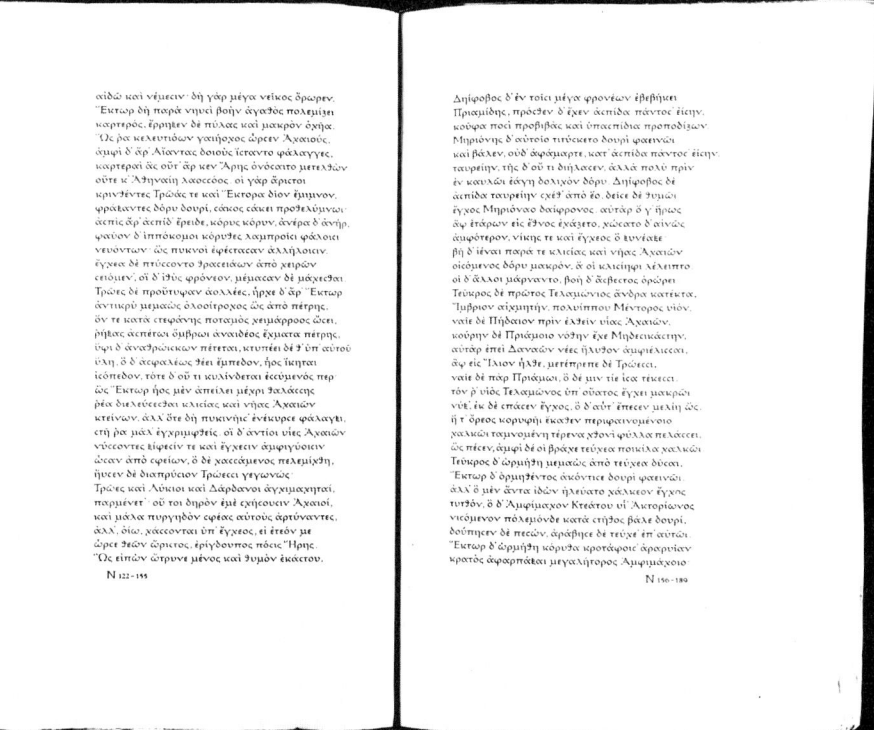

PLATE 42

Her approach to the design of the canto headings is very close to Hewitt's, not only in her calligraphic style, but in her vertical arrangement of letters adjacent to the initials. Simon's designs for several Bremer-Presse works were assembled in the portfolio, *Titel und Initialen*, printed from the original blocks in 1926. The self-contained vitality and compositional balance of her designs work beautifully even when isolated from the text. [41]

For his ΙΛΙΑΣ (Iliad), printed in 1923, Wiegand designed a Greek font which maintained the clarity of Aldus's while moving closer to the connected-letter style of Garamond's ligature-filled font. Wiegand designed his *griechische Schrift* along the same principles he followed for his Antiqua, creating variant forms for his uppercase Π and lowercase ι, π, σ, and τ. Most of the variations were designed for letter spacing, like his Antiqua t, and one, ς, to conclude words only. The Bremer-Presse reliance on the combination of pure typography as ornament sufficient to decorate books might have resulted in the severity of the Doves Press. But Wiegand's success in manipulating the nuances of typographic design into flexible, script-like fonts of type, allowed him to capture something of the subtle variety and shifting cadences of handwritten manuscripts in the Bremer-Presse editions. [42]

Kessler · The Cranach-Presse

Count Harry Kessler was an impresario among the publishers of the early twentieth century. Like his friend Diaghilev, the Russian organizer of the Ballets Russes, Kessler brought together an international group of leading graphic artists, type designers, and pressmen to form his Cranach-Presse, the source of some of the most artistic books of its generation.

Born in Paris and educated in England and Germany, Kessler (1868–1937) was a prominent German politician, diplomat, and patron whose travels brought him into contact with major figures in the arts. The idea for his press came during one of Kessler's many trips abroad. About 1908 he invited the French sculptor Aristide Maillol (1861–1944) to join him on a trip to Greece. Moved by this ancient culture, the two began discussing the creation of illustrated editions of classical literature.

Maillol's work for one of these editions, Virgil's *Eclogae*, though begun in 1912, was not completed until 1926 because of the war. Maillol is known primarily for the classical restraint of his figure sculptures, and this economy of means led to a realization of sculpture as a pure art form, stripped of literary or artistic associations. His illustrations for the *Eclogae* are characteristic in their archaic simplicity and elemental power, expressed through his use of "naive" compositions and "primitive" line. The layout follows Morris's style, but the space surrounding the illustrations and type has been enlarged considerably, transforming it from an arrangement of margins into a picture frame. The type, designed for the Cranach-Presse by Emery Walker, is yet another version of Jenson and virtually identical to Walker's design for the Doves type. [43]

Edward Gordon Craig (1872–1966), an Englishman, was a controversial theorist, actor, director, and designer of the twentieth-century stage. His efforts centered on productions in which the actors' performances as well as the scenery were structured to evoke rather than explain the literary content of a play. Kessler first approached Craig for illustrations to a Cranach *Hamlet* in 1912, but this project was also interrupted by the war and not completed until 1929. The raw markings, which only allude to forms and relationships, reverse the conventional arrangement of illustration and text. The text no longer provides a setting for the illustration, rather the illustration has absorbed the text, making the typography part of the texture of the image. The Gothic-style type, first used in this edition, was designed for the Cranach-Presse by Edward Johnston. Drawn with close reference to one of the earliest movable types, the lowercase letters remain generally faithful to the jagged character of the fifteenth-century Germanic model. The uppercase letters, however, are independent creations which tend toward gothicised versions of the erect, inscriptional forms of Roman epigraphy. One unusual feature is the deformed uppercase H designed with a shorter stem on the right than the left. [44]

An English illustrator, type designer, engraver, and sculptor, Eric Gill (1882–1940) had engraved a number of titles and initials for the Cranach-Presse, before illustrating the *Canticum canticorum Salomonis*, printed

43. Virgil. *Eclogae*. Trans. by Rudolf Alexander Schröder. Weimar: Cranach-Presse, 1926. Illustrations by Aristide Maillol; title and initial letters design by Eric Gill; initial letter ornaments design by Aristide Maillol; roman type design by Emery Walker; italic type design by Edward Johnston; book design by Harry Kessler. No. 155 of 250. 32.5 × 24 cm.

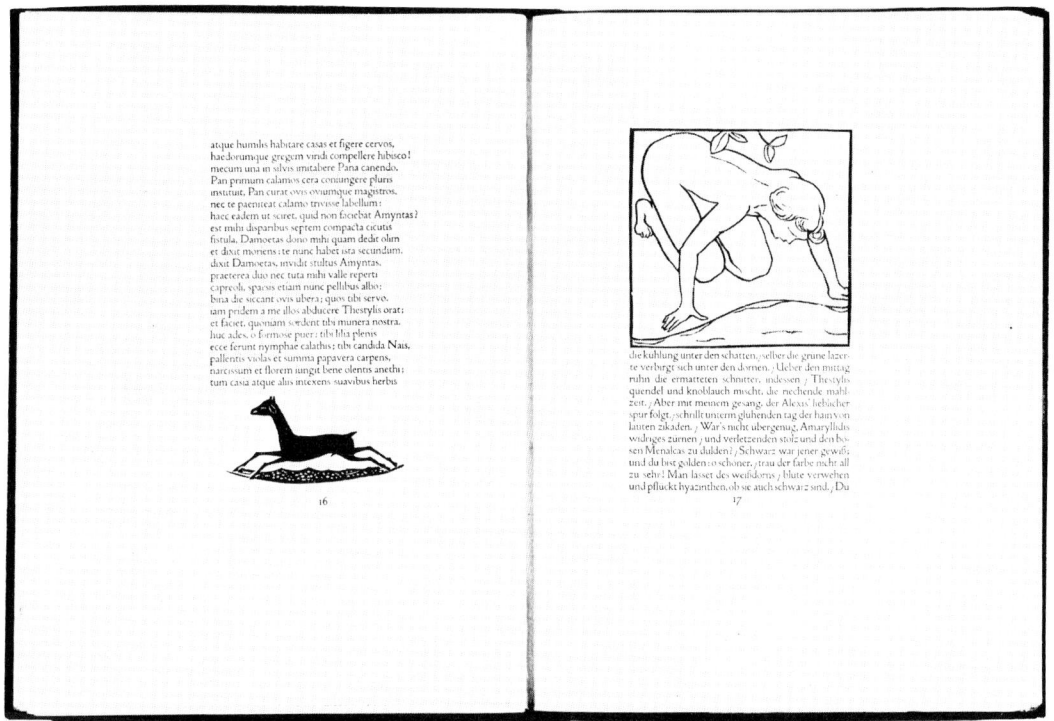

PLATE 43

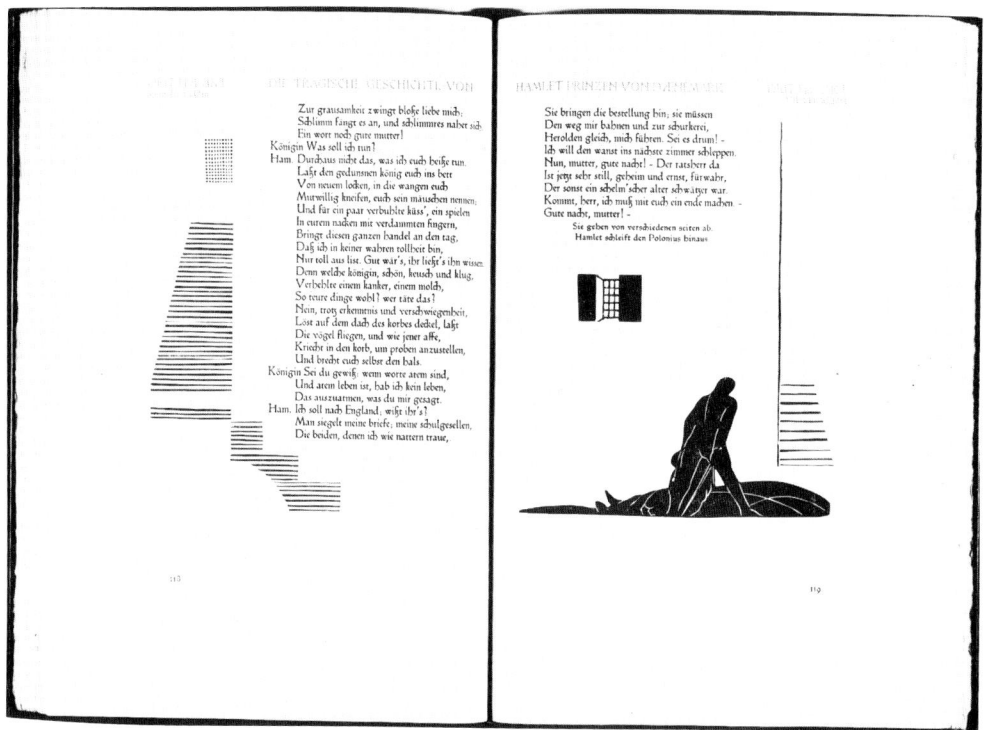

PLATE 44

in 1931. The softly rounded figures modeled in shallow spaces are characteristic of Gill's lyrical compositions, the negative shading along the contours of the forms creating an eerie atmosphere. The wood engravings are printed with two colors: black over a creamy, almost imperceptible off-white. The light coloring was probably intended to both add some warmth to the metallic rendering of the engravings, as well as glaze the paper to provide a smooth saturated surface for the black. A comparison with the black-only impression in the specimen reveals that, without the underglazing, the black ink is absorbed into the paper resulting in a grey, lifeless image. The sharp contrast of these dark illustrations is critical to this exotic, and oftentimes erotic rendering of the text. Consistent with the other Cranach-Presse books, the relationship of image to text is designed to supplant a benign "picturing" of the narrative with images that tend more to confront than interpret the text in a continuing tension-filled visual dialogue. [45, 46]

44. William Shakespeare. *Die tragische Geschichte von Hamlet Prinzen von Daenemark*. Trans. by Gerhart Hauptmann. Weimar: Cranach-Presse, 1927–1929. Illustrations by Edward Gordon Craig; title page design by Eric Gill; type design by Edward Johnston; book design by Harry Kessler. No. 5 of 230. 36.1 × 24.5 cm.

45. *Canticum canticorum Salomonis*. Weimar: Cranach-Presse, 1931. Illustrations and initials designed by Eric Gill; roman type design by Emery Walker; italic type design by Edward Johnston; book design by Harry Kessler. No. 117 of 200. 26.1 × 13.6 cm.

46. *Canticum canticorum Salomonis*. [Specimen page.] Weimar: Cranach-Presse, 1931. Illustration and initials designed by Eric Gill; type design by Emery Walker; page design by Harry Kessler. Not published as presented. 25.5 × 12.8 cm.

PLATE 45

PLATE 46

Some Books on Printing and Design

Introduction

The materials which follow were used by printers to understand and solve routine problems of printing and design. These include technical manuals, specimens of type designs, design idea books, and runs of trade journals. Many of the books illustrate specific processes, and a number reflect alternative solutions to the special design and production problems in children's literature and books on art and photography. Ephemera, such as automobile brochures and travel promotions, were consulted for current ideas on the treatment of specific advertising topics.

Selected with an eye to the richness and diversity of the commercial printer's world, there are practical books such as Alois Senefelder's historic *Complete Course of Lithography*, and somewhat less practical books such as the delightful *Achievement in Photo-Engraving* with its pages of candy wrappers. A few finely printed books are here as well, including Giambattista Bodoni's handsome *Manuale tipografico* and Owen Jones's brilliant, full-color *Illuminated Books of the Middle Ages*.

Most of these books would no longer be useful in a printing shop today. Their interest now lies in their documentation of the history of a complex and rapidly changing technology as well as in their ability to suggest the mood and feel of an earlier time.

Letterpress Printing

The books shown thus far were printed, with one exception, by a technique called letterpress, which remained unchanged from Gutenberg until the mid-nineteenth century. It is called letterpress because it is primarily used for printing text. The process consists of essentially three steps: first the type, pieces of metal about one inch long with raised letters on the end (similar in appearance to the letters on the ends of typewriter keys), is arranged in rectangular frames with the letters up; next, the ink is applied to the raised surfaces of the letters; and last, a sheet of paper is laid over the type and pressure is applied with a press to force the paper into contact with the type, transferring the ink to the paper.

A thorough account of letterpress techniques and equipment is contained in John Johnson's *Typographia, or, the Printers' Instructor*, published in 1824. Johnson (1777–1848), an English printer who headed his own press, set aside the first of his two-volume *Typographia* for a general history of printing. In it he discusses the Chinese origins of printing, as well as Gutenberg and the spread of printing through the Low Countries and England. [47] The second volume includes a survey of contemporary printing equipment and practices along with an extensive illustrated discussion of Oriental alphabets and a printer's glossary. Johnson devotes a portion of the volume to a review of recent advances in press design and construction. One of the major improvements of the time was the use of iron in place of wood for the major structural elements of the press, and one of the most popular of the new iron presses was

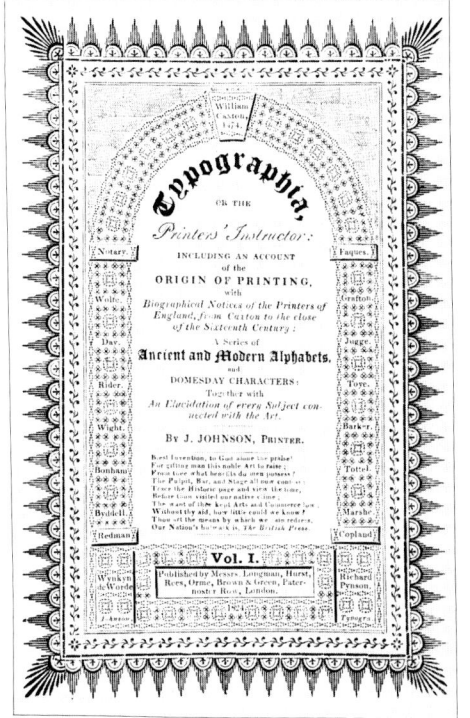

PLATE 47

PLATE 48

designed by an American, George Clymer (1754–1834). Clymer's Columbian Press, with an ingenious counter-balanced lever assembly, could exert many times more pressure than a wooden press and thus give clearer impressions with much less effort. Johnson apparently favored this press above the others he studied—he purchased two Columbians for his shop, eventually using them to print the work shown here. [48]

The basic principle behind letterpress printing is used in inkless stamping or embossing. The technique is essential in creating texts for the blind, one of seventeen hundred topics arranged alphabetically in

---

47,48. John Johnson. *Typographia, or, the Printers' Instructor.* London: Longman, Hurst, et al., 1824. 23 × 15 cm.

49. *American Encyclopaedia of Printing.* Ed. by J. Luther Ringwalt. Philadelphia: Menamin and Ringwalt, 1871. 26.9 × 20 cm.

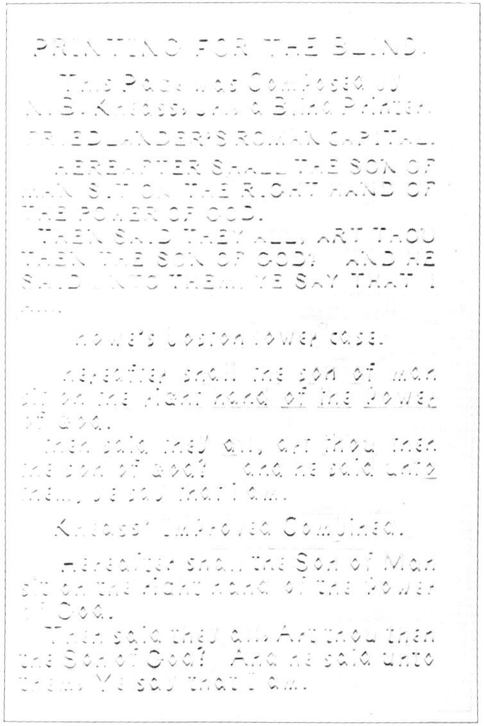

PLATE 49

 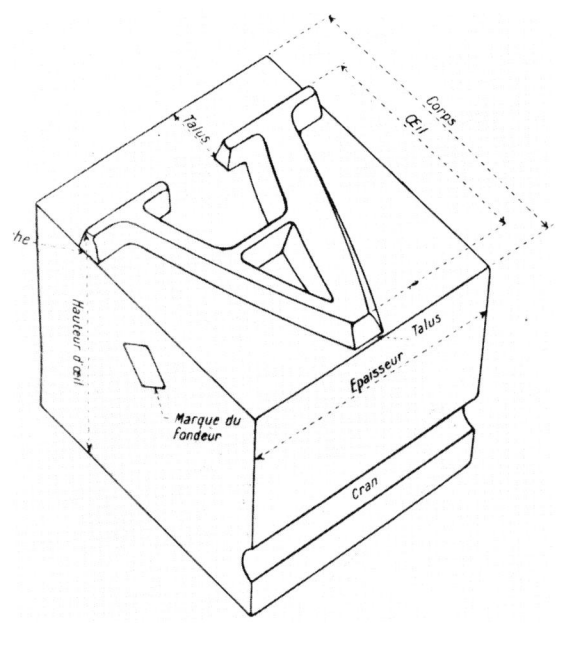

PLATE 50

the *American Encyclopaedia of Printing*. Printed in 1871, the *Encyclopaedia* was edited by J. Luther Ringwalt from an English compendium. Ringwalt and his wife, however, contributed numerous additions and solicited the help of experts for other entries as well. One of these, a Philadelphia publisher and printer of a magazine for the sightless, wrote "Printing for the Blind." After presenting an historical background, the article discusses contemporary methods of printing for the blind, a matter of some controversy. The author, who has little use for the Braille method, classifying it as "arbitrary," advocates "alphabetical" systems and has included an embossed sample of his "Kneass' Improved Combined." [49]

Letterpress today has virtually ceased as a commercially viable method of printing. However, it persists as the dominant medium for most finely printed books. *La typographie* (1930), written by the French author and bibliophile Marcel Valotaire (b. 1889), is designed to extol and explain the virtues of letterpress. In a step-by-step tour of the process, this work provides a lucid literary and visual explanation of the technique. *La typographie* is itself a work of fine printing, published by a Frenchman who specialized in letterpress, particularly books illustrated with artists' original prints. It is opened to the last of four pages of type specimens on the left, and an enlargement of a single piece of type on the right. The accompanying glassine overlay carries descriptive terminology. [50]

50. Marcel Valotaire. *La typographie*. Paris: Henry Babou, 1930. No. 187 of 1,000. 25.9 × 20.2 cm.

Type Specimens

Since the end of the fifteenth century typefounders, craftsmen who specialize in the design and manufacture of type, have advertised their wares in type specimens. These began as single sheets and later were expanded into books containing impressions of the styles and sizes of types offered by a typefounder. The specimens are generally arranged to display the types available with either a few lines or an entire page of text set in each example to demonstrate how the type would appear when used in a book.

William Caslon (1754–1833) was the third in a line of England's most prominent family of typefounders. Begun by his grandfather in the first quarter of the eighteenth century, the Caslon typefoundry quickly became known for the quality and variety of its typefaces, including Oriental fonts. Each successive generation left its mark, and William Caslon III, the first to be called "Letter-Founder to His Majesty" took a special interest in ornaments. His enthusiasm for "typographical embellishments" shows in this *Specimen of Printing Types* published in 1785. [51] The opposite page carries a number of the Caslon Oriental alphabets along with Caslon Black Letter, the type which Pickering and Whittingham had recast for their 1844 *Book of Common Prayer.* [7]

The unique character of the work of Giambattista Bodoni was in large part

51. William Caslon III. *A Specimen of Printing Types.* [London:] William Caslon III, 1785. 42.1 × 26 cm.

Type Specimens

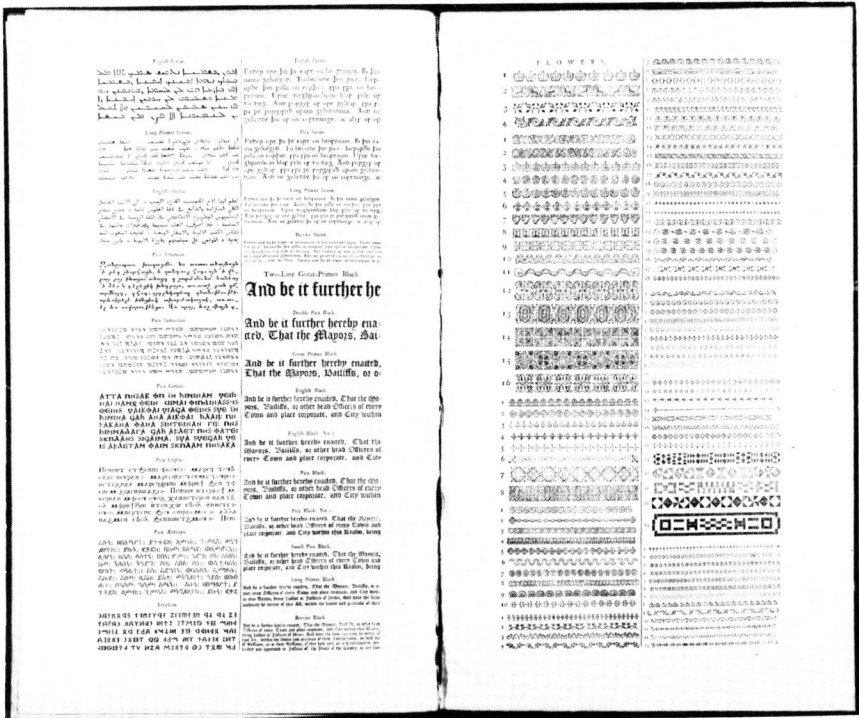

PLATE 51

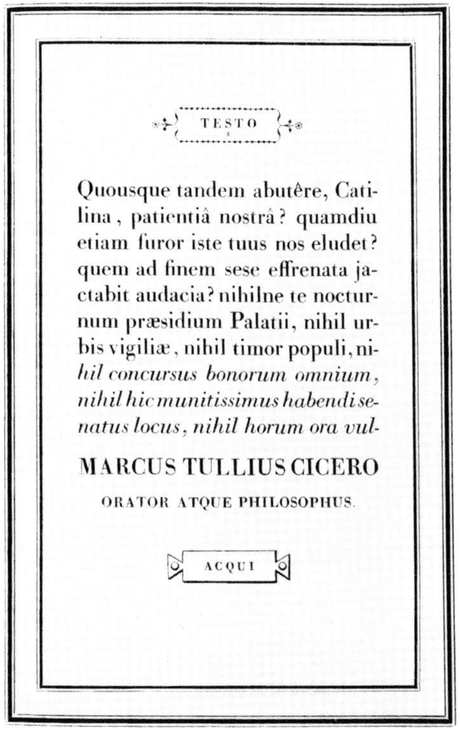

96 Some Books on Printing and Design

PLATE 52

PLATE 53

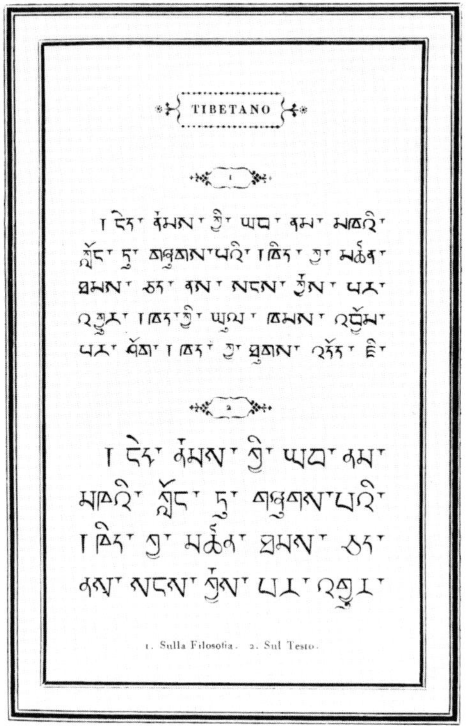

due to his genius as a type designer. Bodoni planned to celebrate his achievement in a huge two-volume collection of specimens which was halted by his death in 1813. Bodoni's widow completed the project five years later, one of the most sumptuous type specimens ever published, containing over two hundred, fifty typefaces and a thousand borders and ornaments. The first volume is devoted to Bodoni's roman and italic faces, the second to foreign alphabets, ornaments, and signs. [52, 53] Bodoni acquired his knowledge of Oriental alphabets while training as a type engraver in the papal missionary center, the Congregatio de Propaganda Fide. The Vatican Congregatio

52,53. Giambattista Bodoni. *Manuale tipografico.* Parma: Presso La Vedova, 1818. 32.6 × 22.5 cm.

54. Pierre Didot L'Aîné. *Specimen des nouveaux caractères.* Paris: Pierre Didot L'Aîné et Jules Didot, Fils, 1819. 25.5 × 18 cm.

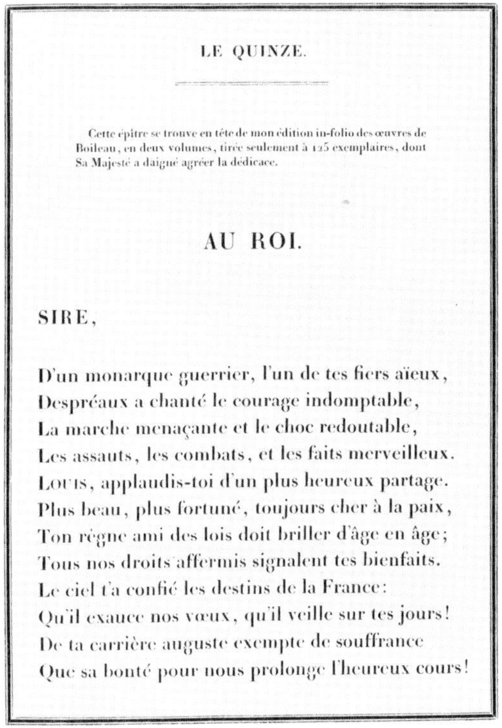

PLATE 54

housed a printing office which was the source of Bibles and other religious texts in native languages used by Catholic missionaries.

Pierre Didot (1761–1853), representing the third generation in the leading typefounding family of France, took over the firm in 1789. Didot was a demanding and meticulous craftsman. He wrote in the introduction to *Specimen des nouveaux caractères* (1819) of how he hoped to bring his types "to perfection," making sure that his "directions . . . [were] carried out with the utmost fidelity, as well as all ideas for improvements, sometimes resulting in the same font being cut three and four times over again." Didot also believed that the common practice of identifying different sizes of type with names was needlessly confusing. He was among the first to attempt to clarify matters by devising a standard numbering system to give the sizes of his types. Didot's method, used in this specimen book, is still followed today. [54]

Goudy · Type Design

Frederic W. Goudy was a leading participant in the typographic renaissance at the turn of the century, and he became one of this nation's most prolific free-lance type designers. Through his work as an author, Goudy argued tirelessly for the adoption of high standards by the American printing industry.

Goudy designed over one hundred typefaces, several of which remain in use today. Most of his work was sold to typefounders who, by the beginning of the twentieth century, were turning increasingly to independent designers for fresh ideas. The use of contemporary designers stemmed from an interest in quality typography stimulated by the modern fine printing movement, of which Goudy's Village Press was a leading example. One of Goudy's first and largest customers was the American Type Founders Company, which devoted an entire specimen book to a selection of Goudy types. [55] Another client was the Lanston Monotype Machine Company which developed typefaces exclusively for its machines, including designs by Goudy. [56] The Lanston Company employed Goudy's talents in other ways as well: first, as Art Director from 1920 to 1939, and then as Typographic Counsel.

Nearly all of Goudy's typographic designs were collected in his *Half Century of Type Design and Typography* printed in two

55. *A Composite Showing of Goudy Types.* Jersey City, New Jersey: American Type Founders Company, 1927. 31 × 23.9 cm.

56. *Goudy Text & Lombardic Capitals.* Philadelphia: Lanston Monotype Machine Company, [1931]. 31.1 × 23.5 cm.

Some Books on Printing and Design

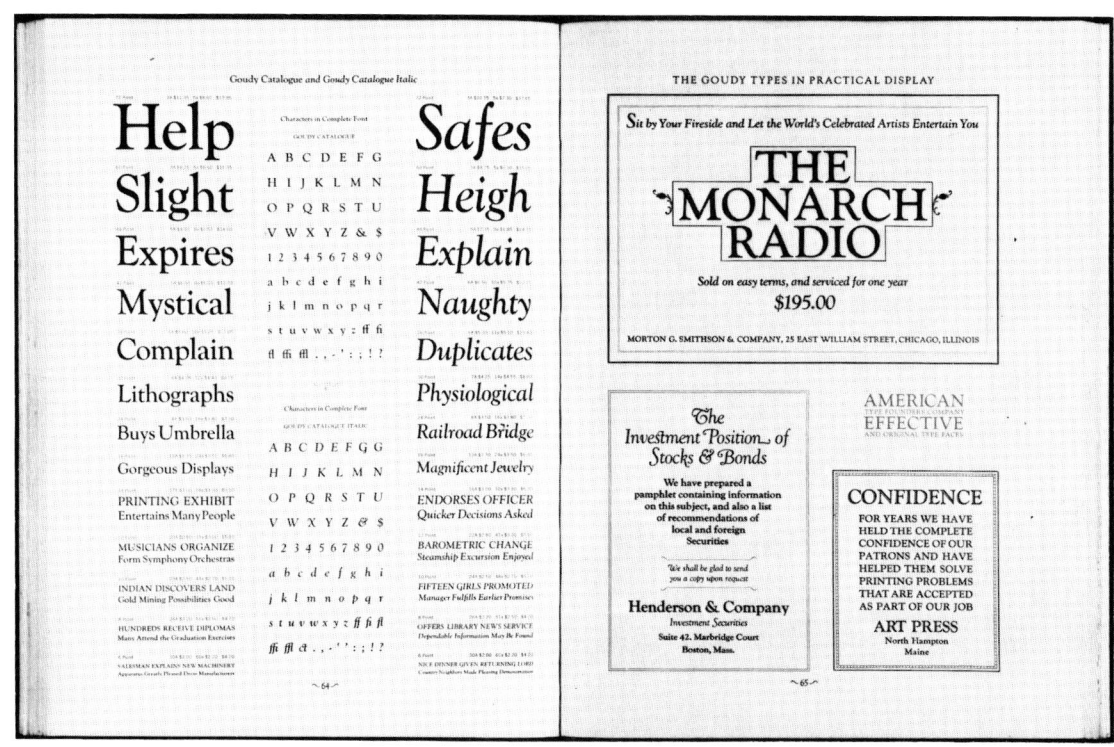

PLATE 55

Goudy · Type Design　　　101

PLATE 56

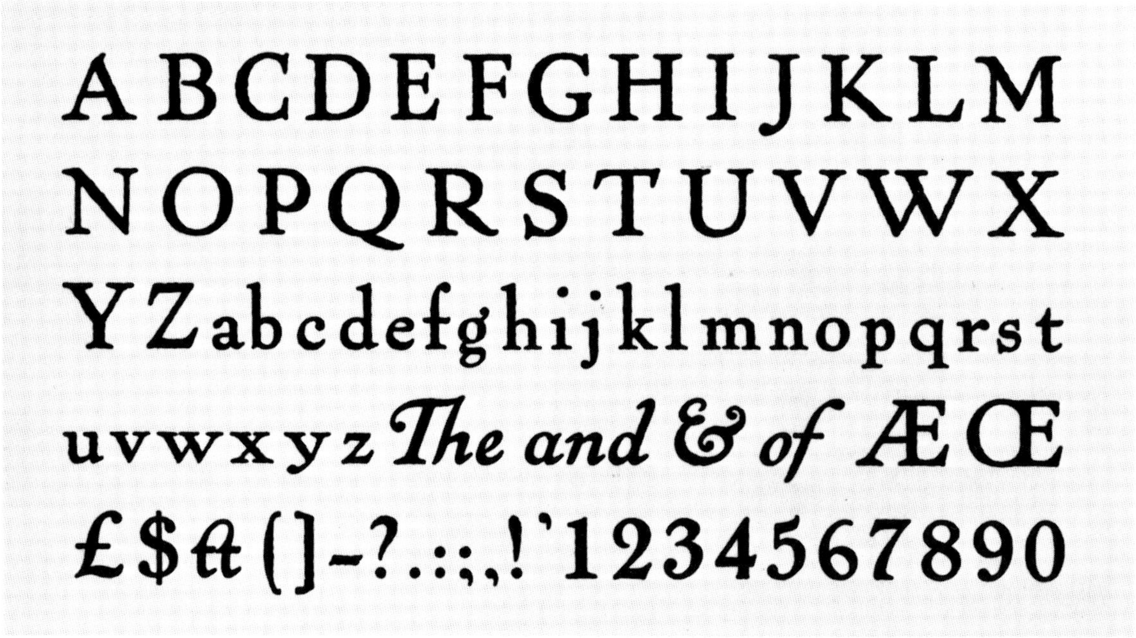

ABCDEFGHIJKLM
NOPQRSTUVWX
YZabcdefghijklmnopqrst
uvwxyz *The and & of* ÆŒ
£$ ft ()-?.:;,!'1234567890

PLATE 57

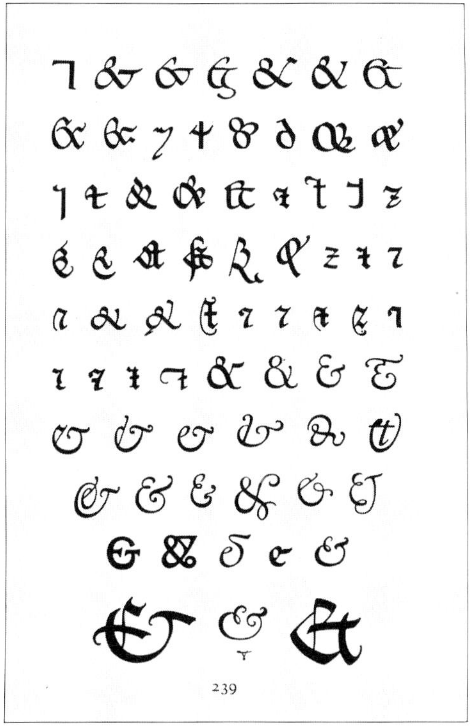

PLATE 58

239

volumes in 1946. The set includes reproductions of his types beginning with his earliest fonts—such as this design for the Pabst Brewing Company—which were created for firms in the Chicago area, where Goudy began his career. [57] Many of Goudy's designs were based on a lively historical curiosity which often turned in unexpected ways. One unusual project was his study of ampersands, partially represented here. [58]

Goudy's leadership in promoting fine typography was not confined to his role as a craftsman. He was the author or editor of more than twenty publications and wrote some thirty-five articles. *Ars Typographica,* "an occasional miscellany of the printing art" founded in 1918 and edited by Goudy, covered all aspects of the graphic arts. An

57,58. Frederic W. Goudy. *A Half Century of Type Design and Typography.* New York: The Typophiles, 1946. No. 369 of 825. 19.5 × 12.1 cm.

inexpensively produced periodical, it was intended to advance quality design and printing through its example as well as its content:

A book need not be badly printed in order to bring it within reasonable cost of manufacture. Even cheap paper, inexpensive inks, mechanical composition, do not preclude the well-designed page or good type design, since they cost no more than bad, and the difference in effect is out of all proportion to any slight difference in cost that their use and a little more care and thought might involve. [59]

One of Goudy's most instructive books is his *Typologia*, published in 1940. Partially a collection of unpublished essays, the book

---

59. *Ars Typographica.* Vol. I, no. 3. Spring, 1920. Ed. by Frederic W. Goudy. New York: The Marchbanks Press. 32.2 × 21 cm.

60. Frederic W. Goudy. *Typologia.* Berkeley: University of California Press, 1940. Unnumbered copy of edition of three hundred, signed by the author. 27.5 × 18 cm.

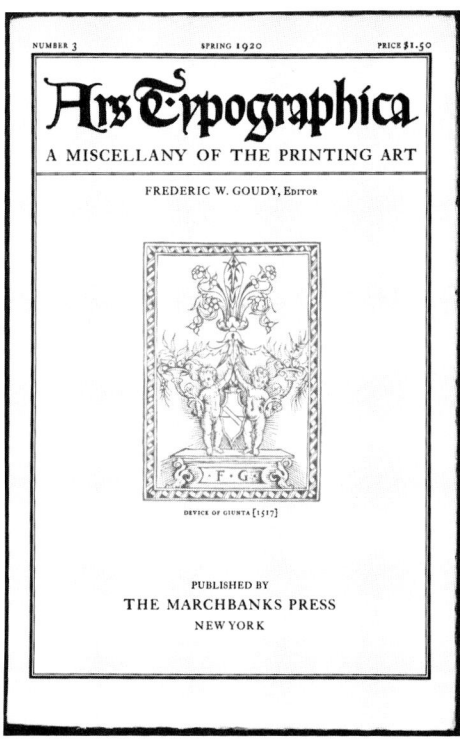

PLATE 59

[86   TYPOLOGIA

I find it is well to lay them aside for a few days and then go over them again with a fresh eye; minor discrepancies overlooked in the glow of creation show up plainly now and are easily rectified. But I do not think a design should be gone over again and again, as this tends to tighten and stiffen it, to kill the spontaneity of handling that is so desirable. To do this par-

DEEPDENE ITALIC, MEDIAEVAL, VILLAGE NO. 2, GOUDY TEXT, AND GOETHE, ALL DRAWN TO SAME SCALE. VERTICAL LINES SHOW FITTING OF EACH CHARACTER. TOP AND BOTTOM LINES REPRESENT THE TYPE BODY.

ticular design as well as I can at the moment and to do the next one better, if possible, has been my rule for years.

No rule can be given for determining the relative weights of stem, hairline, or serif, nor for the relative height of "middles" and "ascenders"—they are interdependent, although these items may be indicated somewhat by the intended use of the face. It is difficult also to visualize a type design as type from a large drawing. In my own work I usually have in mind in general the character and weight I wish to produce, and I

DETAILS OF CONSTRUCTION   87]

have so many drawings* in the same scale on hand that have actually been made into type that it is a simple matter to say roughly "a shade heavier in stem than some one of these, or with hairlines lighter, or serifs stronger, or the bowls rounder, or more oval, or the general effect more condensed or blacker

VILLAGE NO. 2 AND GOETHE, ILLUSTRATING DIFFERENCES IN STEMS, SERIFS, DESCENDERS, AND BOWLS

or lighter," and with the dimensions of these drawings already exhibited in types made from them I begin with certain things already pretty well established. It is then that drawing begins. Capitals must not be unnecessarily self-assertive, or they will "spot" the page. A little difference in width of stem—a difference that may be measured only by a micrometer microscope in the type itself—will change the color of a printed page, and I am of the opinion that the wished-for weight is

* These words were written before the destruction by fire of my entire plant and equipment on January 26, 1939.

includes discussions of the "Invention of Typography," "The First Types," "Legibility," and "Fine Printing." The central concerns of *Typologia*, however, are the aesthetic issues and mechanical limitations facing a type designer. These are presented in language free of technical jargon accessible to anyone interested in learning how printing type is designed and produced. [60]

Color Printing · Letterpress & Stencil

Color printing was produced on a limited basis from the fifteenth to the early nineteenth centuries when attempts at significantly expanding and refining the process began to occur. The underlying principle which remained the same throughout this period was simple. Images were made up of 'local' colors so that, in a hypothetical picture, for a leaf a green ink is used, for the sky a blue, for a flower a yellow, and so on. Consequently, in a complicated image of twenty or thirty colors an equal number of inks had to be mixed, and often an equal number of printing blocks prepared to apply the ink.

Seeking to improve this process, William Savage summarized the results of several years of experimentation in his *Practical Hints on Decorative Printing*, which he advertised as

. . . . a PRACTICAL WORK, addressed to the PROFESSED PRINTER—it will contain Instructions for forming the finest Black and Coloured Inks, embellished with numerous Engravings on Wood by the first Artists; to serve not only as Specimens of the Different Inks, but also as Specimens of Ornamental Printing.

A one-time superintendent of the printing office of England's Royal Institution, Savage (1770–1843) completed *Practical Hints* in 1823, after seven years of intense labor and crippling expenses. Based on tests in the formulation and manufacture of printing inks, Savage's work is most useful for its chapters "On Printing Materials," "Presswork," and "On Printing in Colours." Along with several pages of color ink samples are specimens of color printing, including "Ode to Mercy," shown here. The image was printed with thirty hues applied by twenty-nine wood printing blocks. [61]

A step-by-step sequence of color proofs from Hans Alexander Mueller's *Woodcuts & Wood Engravings: How I Make Them* (1939) reveals how Savage and his predecessors created images through the use of 'local' colors. Mueller (b. 1888), a

61. William Savage. *Practical Hints on Decorative Printing.* London: Longman, Hurst, Rees, [etc.], 1816–1823. Bound with: "Proposals for Publishing by Subscription, Practical Hints on Decorative Printing." Lambeth: William Savage, March, 1816; printed cover letter "With this I transmit the Prospectus . . ." Lambeth: William Savage, April, 1816; prospectus "Practical Hints on Decorative Printing." Brunswick Square: W. Savage, November, 1818. 28.5 × 22.6 cm.

62. Hans Alexander Mueller. *Woodcuts & Wood Engravings: How I Make Them.* New York: Pynson Printers, 1939. Edition: 3000. 32.8 × 25.5 cm.

PLATE 61

Color Printing · Letterpress & Stencil 109

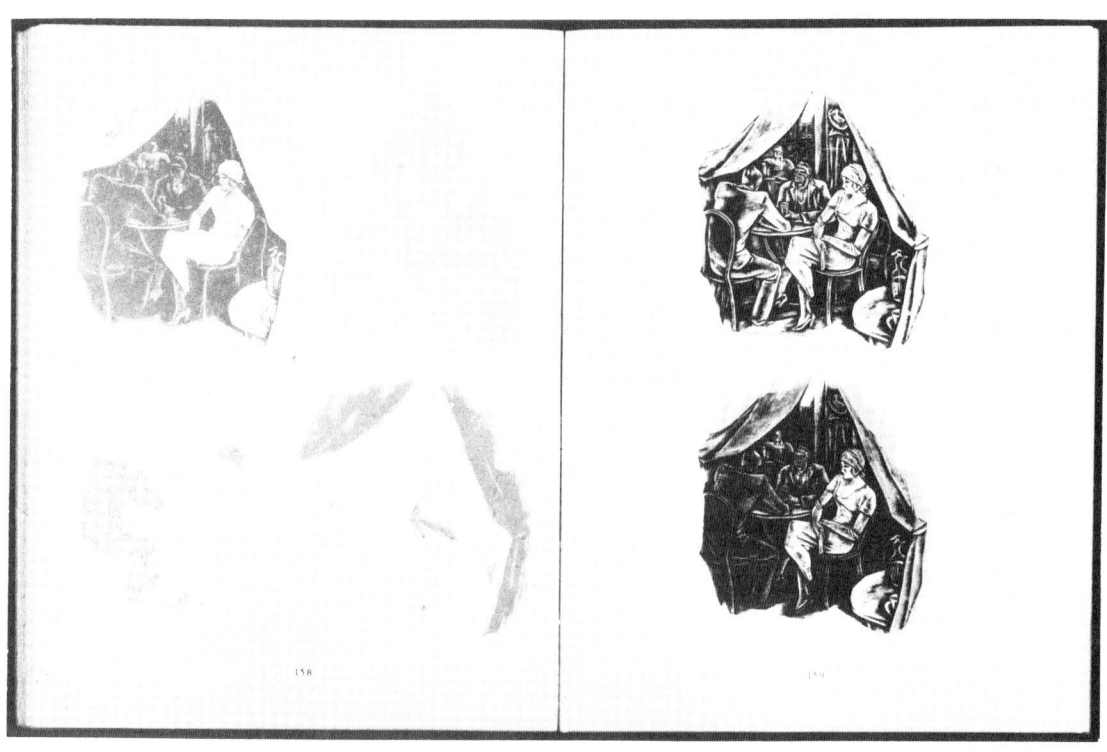

PLATE 62

110 Some Books on Printing and Design

PLATE 63

German engraver and illustrator who emigrated to America, demonstrated his color technique by printing a color illustration along with a separate impression of each of the five colors used in the completed image. Shown here, the colors were printed one by one, beginning with the upper left-hand corner of the left page and moving left to right, top to bottom, the color at the top of the right-hand page added last. [62] This approach, however, required enormous labor, particularly in elaborate productions such as Savage's "Ode"; as the cost of labor increased the process was rendered useless for commercial purposes.

The dominant commercial color printing method today came out of a series of developments which began in the late nineteenth century. It is based on photomechanical separations of colors usually printed in four hues. But these are not printed in solid tones such as found in the work of Savage and Mueller, and are seldom 'local.' Rather, the colors, usually variations on the three primary hues (red, yellow, blue) plus black, are printed in patterns of tiny dots arranged to blend optically, creating the appearance of a full spectrum of colors. In the image described earlier, the sky would be printed with blue ink and the balloon with yellow ink; but the leaf would be printed with a combination of yellow and blue dots which, at normal viewing distance, would blend to give the impression of a green, thereby eliminating one color and one printing block required to print it. A two page exhibit from *The Advertising and Publishing Production Yearbook*, issued in 1937 and intended as a guide to the latest techniques and services available in the printing industry, demonstrates this color process.

63. *The Advertising and Publishing Production Yearbook*. Ed. by Eugene M. Ettenberg. New York: Leo H. Joachim, 1937. 28.9 × 22 cm.

112   Some Books on Printing and Design

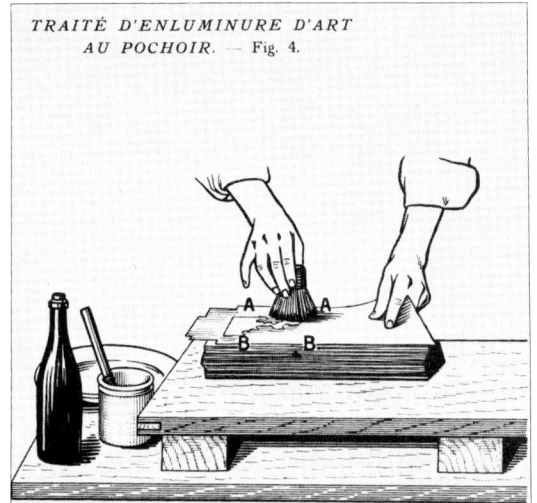

PLATE 64

PLATE 65

The left-hand page shows a four-color illustration printed in the same way as most current news magazines and periodicals, but enlarged several times to show the color dot patterns. The facing page shows separations of the four colors used to print the illustration in the left column, and how the illustration looked after each successive hue was added in the right column. The text gives a detailed explanation of the process. [63]

Jean Saudé's *Traité d'enluminure d'art au pochoir*, printed in 1925, outlines the stencil method for creating multiple color images. Based on a centuries-old method for coloring fabrics, the technique requires cutting stencils out of heavy, coated papers—one for each color—through which the ink is daubed or brushed. In a series of fourteen steps, Saudé demonstrated the basic technique as well as some special variations. [64] Saudé also included over twenty color plates illustrating the special thickness and corresponding opacity of the ink which can be achieved by this method. [65] Since the Second World War this process has become important in the printing of a number of commercial products ranging from decals to t-shirts. Now called serigraphy, or silkscreen, because the stencils are attached to silk-like meshes through which the ink is squeegeed, the process has also come to be used in the way Saudé envisioned: as a printing technique for the work of many contemporary artists.

64,65. Jean Saudé. *Traité d'enluminure d'art au pochoir.* Paris: Éditions de l'Ibis, 1925. No. 241 of 475. Signed by the author. 33.1 × 25.5 cm.

Color Printing · Lithography

Lithography, which had a significant impact on the development of nineteenth century color printing and illustration, was invented in 1798 by Alois Senefelder. An aspiring but not altogether successful German playwright, Senefelder (1771–1834) set out to invent a simplified process, relatively unencumbered by equipment, to print his work. Senefelder's discovery is based on the chemical resistance of oil to water: first one marks a specially prepared stone slab with a greasy crayon or ink to create the design to be printed; then the stone is chemically treated to fix the image to the stone and sensitize the unmarked or 'negative' areas to maintain a film of water; next the stone is dampened, holding moisture in the 'negative' areas; ink is then rolled over the stone sticking to the receptive 'positive' areas and resisted by the dampened 'negative' areas; last, a sheet of paper is laid over the stone and the two are cranked through a press to transfer, under pressure, the ink to the sheet. The illustration, printed by this method, shows one of three different types of manual lithographic presses pictured in Senefelder's *Complete Course of Lithography*. Published in 1819, it is an authorized translation of Senefelder's two-part historical account and technical explanation of his invention. [66].

Owen Jones (1809–1874), an architect and student of architectural ornament, could not locate a firm willing or able to print an edition of his large, intricately detailed and colored drawings. Jones found

66. Alois Senefelder. *A Complete Course of Lithography*. Trans. by A. S. London: Rudolf Ackerman, 1819. 27.5 × 22 cm.

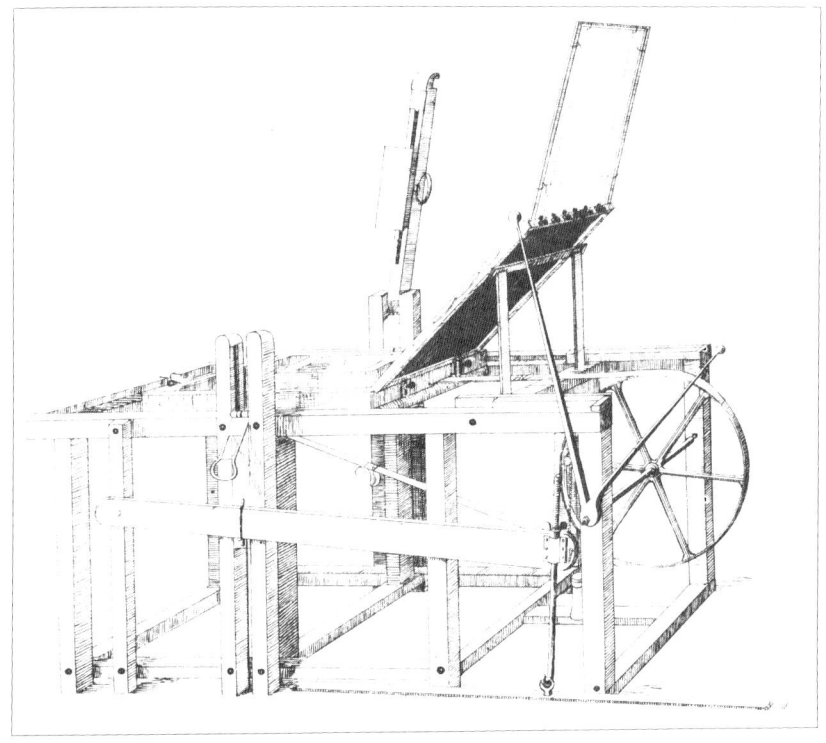

PLATE 66

PLATE 67

in Senefelder's process the capacity to produce the images he envisioned by making drawings directly on the stone. As a result, Jones set up a shop where he adapted the lithographic technique to produce elaborate color or chromolithographs pulled from his own renderings. *The Illuminated Books of the Middle Ages* (1849), which is characteristic of the fine printing and luscious color of Jones's work, was a collaborative effort with another major figure in English color printing, Henry Noel Humphreys (1810–1879), who wrote the text. The initial and ornament on the left and illuminated page on the right were both copied by Jones from a fifteenth-century psalter and, like the other illustrations in this edition, printed

67. Henry Noel Humphreys. *The Illuminated Books of the Middle Ages.* London: Longman, Brown, Green, and Longmans, 1849. Facsimiles copied from the originals and printed by Owen Jones. 56.1 × 38 cm.

actual-size. Jones's color method, based on 'local' color, required dozens of lithographic stones to create each image. This approach was abandoned by commercial printers in favor of the four-color separation method and not revived until the late 1950s as a medium for printing contemporary art, and then, on a vastly reduced scale. [67]

The *Darmstädter Pessach Haggadah*, printed in 1928, is a facsimile reproduction based on essentially the same process as Jones's *Illuminated Books.* While Jones had to prepare a separate stone for each color, the plates for the *Haggadah* were produced photomechanically by a variation of the four-color separation method. The combination of the four-color technique with the capacity for detailed reproduction of the lithographic process enabled the printers to achieve an accurate reproduction of the manuscript. The fac-

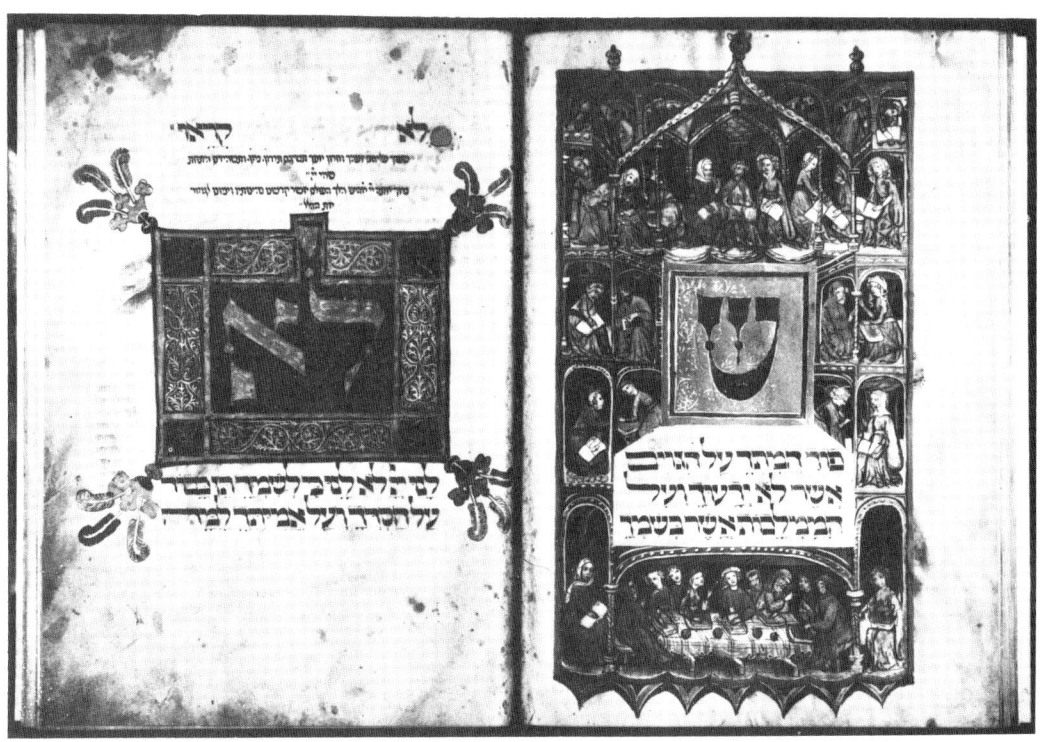

PLATE 68

simile is so faithful that even the imperfections of the fifteenth-century original have been preserved. [68]

A display of technical bravura, the *Darmstädter Haggadah* also represents commercially viable photolithographic techniques used to produce most color printing today—from cereal boxes to fine art reproductions.

68. *Die Darmstädter Pessach-Haggadah.* Facsimile reproduction of Codex Orientalis 8 in the Landesbibliothek zu Darmstadt. Leipzig: Karl W. Hiersemann, 1928. No. 111 of 350. 35.5 × 25.5 cm.

Ruzicka · Color Illustration

For the illustrator the problem of color printing is one of understanding the possibilities and limitations of the processes available. In addition, a knowledge of theories about the physical properties of light and color can be useful, whether to capture effects from nature, or to create eye-catching advertisements. Rudolph Ruzicka was an illustrator who, specializing in color work, expanded his professional interest in the subject to include studies of the history and theory of color in printing.

Ruzicka (1883–1978), born in Czechoslovakia, studied art and design at the Art Institute of Chicago and wood engraving on his own, before settling on the East Coast where he illustrated books for the Merrymount Press among others. Ruzicka's historical interest in color was evident as early as 1915, the year *New York* was published with his color wood engravings. [69] The foreword by him, titled "A Note on the Historical Development of Colour Printing from Wood Engravings," traces the evolution of color printing from Gutenberg to the exposition of the "Societé de la Gravure sur Bois Originale" (1912) which contained samples of Ruzicka's work. The il-

69. Walter Prichard Eaton. *New York*. Intro. by Rudolph Ruzicka. New York: The Grolier Club, 1915. Illustrations designed and engraved by Rudolph Ruzicka; book design by Rudolph Ruzicka; full-page illustrations printed by Emile Fequet; balance of book and illustrations printed by De Vinne Press. Edition: 250. 29.5 × 20 cm.

70. Christmas card for Neva and Guy Littell. [Artist's proof "for imposition of type."] [n.p:] Neva and Guy Littell, 1933. Illustration by Rudolph Ruzicka. 20.5 × 15 cm.

PLATE 69

PLATE 70

PLATE 71

PLATE 72

lustrations for *New York* demonstrate both Ruzicka's command of color and his style, which tends toward subtle manipulations of closely related pastel hues. [70, 71, 72]

Ruzicka's extensive knowledge of color was employed in the three-volume series *Monographs on Color,* published for printers and designers in 1935. As designer and illustrator for the project, Ruzicka translated theoretical discussions of color phenomena into visual images. The second volume, *Color as Light,* is opened to a section explaining why the sky appears blue and how the same phenomenon causes distant mountains to take on a bluish cast. [73] Ruzicka was familiar with this effect, called "atmospheric perspective," and used it to suggest the distance of an object in a landscape such as the large building in the background of the illustration shown in *New York.* In a suite of miniatures at the conclusion of the third volume—*Color in Use*—Ruzicka illustrated a multiplicity of color relationships and the possible alternatives, opportunities, and pitfalls which can come from working with color. [74]

71. Oscar Wilde. *The Happy Prince and Other Tales.* Stamford, Connecticut: The Overbrook Press, 1936. Illustrations designed and engraved by Rudolph Ruzicka. Edition: 250. 25 × 14.2 cm.

72. *The Engraved & Typographic Work of Rudolph Ruzicka • An Exhibition.* New York: The Grolier Club, 1948. Illustrations designed and engraved by Rudolph Ruzicka; printed by The George Grady Press. Edition: 500. Signed by the artist. 21.5 × 15 cm.

73,74. *A Series of Monographs on Color: Color Chemistry; Color as Light; Color in Use.* New York: The International Printing Ink Corporation, 1935. Illustrations and book design by Rudolph Ruzicka. 28.5 × 22.1 cm.

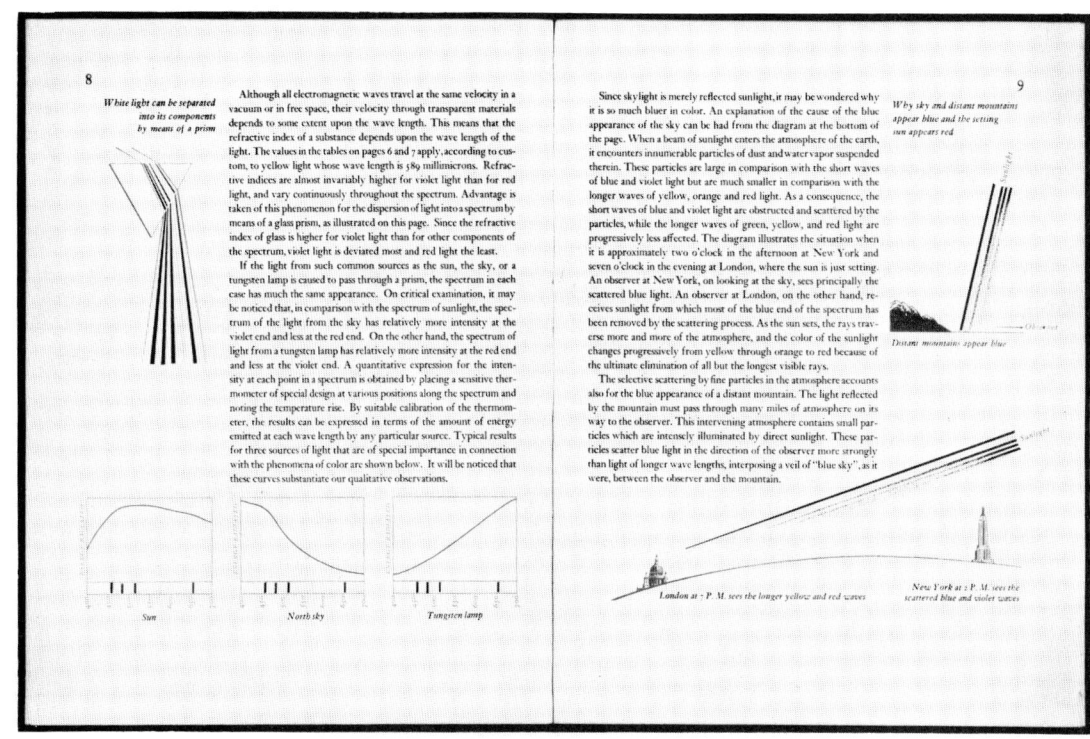

PLATE 73

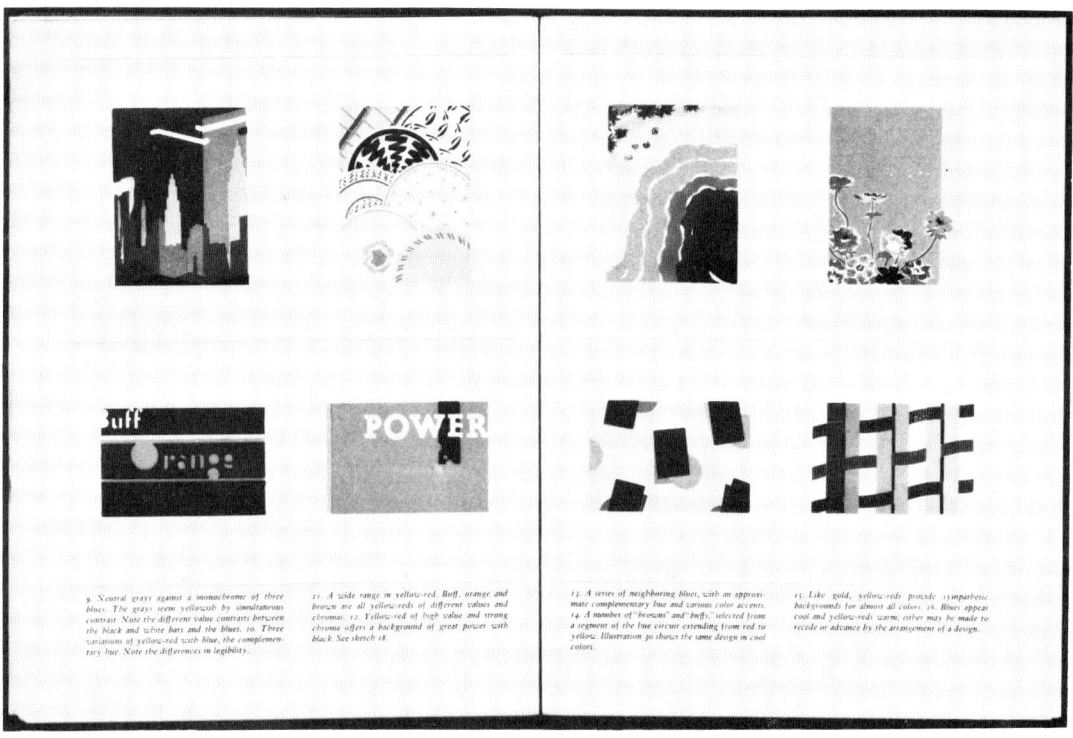

PLATE 74

Journals for the Trade

The growth of the printing industry in the nineteenth century was accompanied by a proliferation of trade magazines and brochures. Primarily designed to advertise printing equipment and supplies, these publications were also instrumental in disseminating new trends in graphic design.

Beginning in 1885, *The American Printer & Bookmaker* ran articles such as "Printing for Profit" and "News of the Trade." The magazine also carried hundreds of ads for presses, paper trimmers, types, and inks, the designs for which were largely stiff and unimaginative. An exception was the series of *art nouveau* advertisements for Ault and Wiborg inks, such as this one published in 1900, which were commissioned to attract attention to its products through advertisements of startling design. [75]

Will Bradley (1868–1962), the designer of the advertisement, began his career in Chicago, with his first recognition coming from magazine covers he created in 1890 for *The Inland Printer* and *Harper's Weekly*. Largely self-taught, Bradley studied the *art nouveau* styles of England and France, particularly the work of a number of artist-designers including William Morris, Aubrey Beardsley, and Henri de Toulouse-Lautrec. Bradley digested these styles and transformed them into a personal approach typified by shallow compositions drawn

75. *The American Printer & Bookmaker.* Vol. XXIX, No. 5. January, 1900. Ed. and published by J. Clyde Oswald. 31 × 22 cm.

Journals for the Trade 127

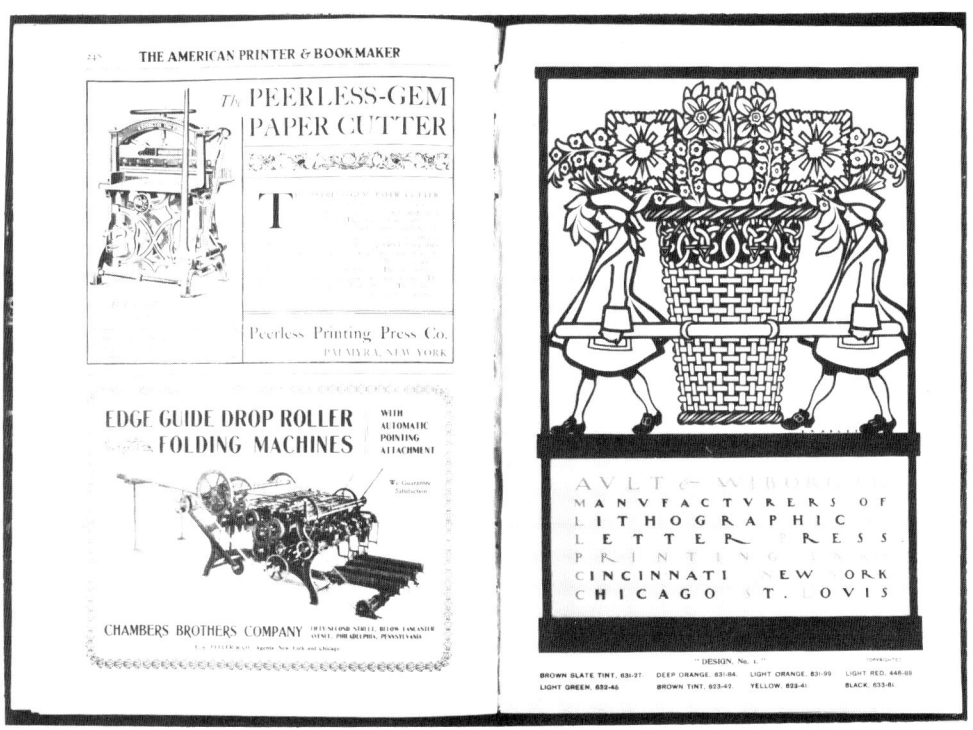

PLATE 75

128 *Some Books on Printing and Design*

PLATE 76

with bold outlines and flat colors. His growing reputation attracted the attention of the American Type Founders Company, which asked Bradley to write and design a series of booklets as promotions for ATF's line of typographic supplies. The immensely successful *American Chap-Book,* published from 1904 through 1905, was the result. It influenced more than a generation of American designers by its use of repeated typographic ornaments to build designs and patterns. Each issue contained a short essay on a design problem ranging from ad layouts to business cards, and was illustrated with a sequence of examples. The issue on "Making Booklets" takes itself as the subject and includes a few tiny pamphlets tipped in. [76] Another issue shows the use of ATF ornaments to create cover designs, listing order numbers and prices at the bottom of the page. [77]

Sources of design ideas for printers grew with the industry in the first quarter of this century. *Westvaco Inspirations for Printers,* for example, which began about 1925, was published by the West Virginia Pulp & Paper Company to promote its Westvaco Mill brand of papers. *Inspirations* was filled with brief pointers for printers, such as the two-page spread shown here from a 1927 issue. [78] Another periodical which often devoted entire issues to a single design topic was the Leipzig *Offset Buch und Werbekunst.* It was established in 1924 to promote a high-speed lithographic pro-

76. *American Chap-Book*. Vol. II. No. 5. July, 1905. Written and designed by Will Bradley; published by American Type Founders Company. 18 × 11 cm.

77. *American Chap-Book*. Vol. I. No. 7. March, 1905. Written and designed by Will Bradley; published by American Type Founders Company. 18 × 11 cm.

78. *Westvaco Inspirations for Printers*. No. 26. 1927. Published by West Virginia Pulp & Paper Company. 31.6 × 24 cm.

130 Some Books on Printing and Design

PLATE 77

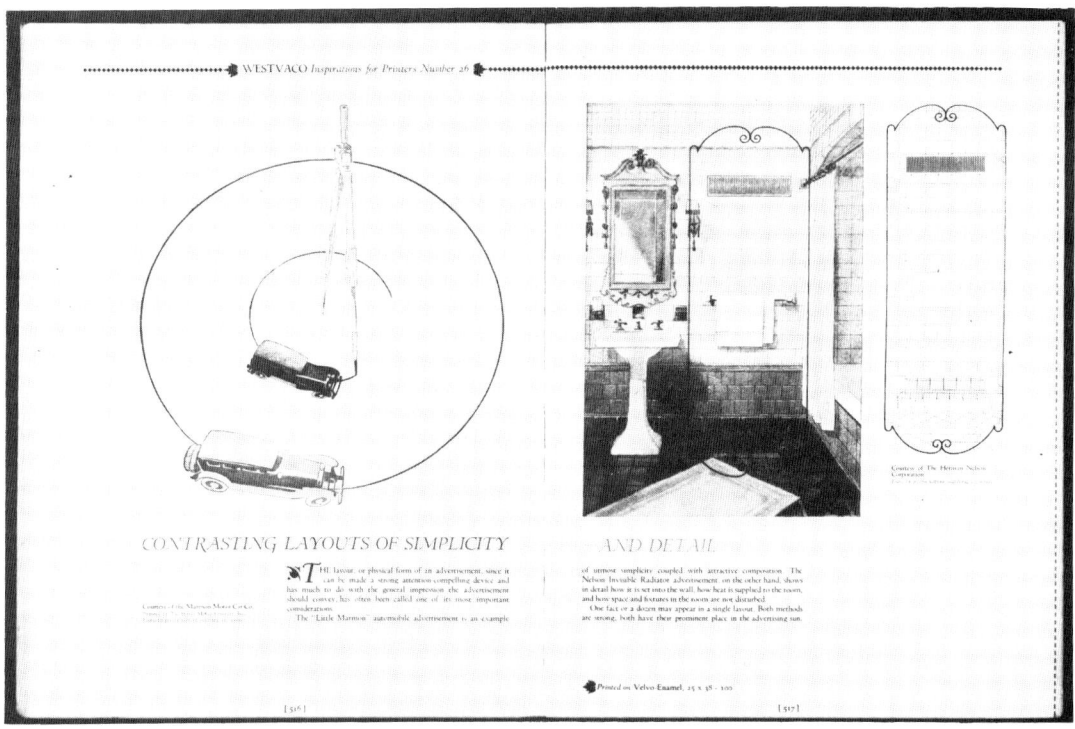

PLATE 78

cess for use in the book and advertising arts. This 1927 issue is devoted almost entirely to a survey of contemporary illustrated children's books. [79]

79. *Offset Buch und Werbekunst.* Vol. IV, No. 10, 1927. Ed. by Siegfried Berg, published by Offset Verlag. 30.6 × 23.6 cm.

PLATE 79

Dwiggins · Printing Design

William Addison Dwiggins, one of America's most original and productive designers, was active in all areas of printing. His work included illustration, calligraphy, and the design of typefaces as well as books.

After studying with Frederic W. Goudy in Chicago, Dwiggins (1880–1956) moved to Massachusetts where he settled as a freelance designer in 1904. His earliest designing often involved magazine advertisements, formats, and mastheads for periodicals such as *Atlantic* and *Life*. The creation of logos was also part of Dwiggins's commercial work. His best-known design is the trademark for General Motors Corporation, still used today largely unchanged.

Dwiggins's illustrations reveal Will Bradley's influence, particularly the latter's use of heavy black outlines and repeated typographic ornaments. Dwiggins's drawings for *Marco Polo* (1933) combine the use of sharp black and white contrasts in pictures bracketed by decorative borders. Characteristic of Dwiggins's style, the borders, appearing to be made up of individual typographic ornaments, are actually part of the illustration. [80]

The design of Dwiggins's title pages for *The Time Machine* (1931) is an intricate

80. Marco Polo. *The Travels of Marco Polo.* Marsden trans. revised and ed. by Manuel Komroff. Rochester, New York: Leo Hart, 1933. Illustrations by William A. Dwiggins. 20.2 × 14.1 cm.

81. H. G. Wells. *The Time Machine.* New York: Random House, 1931. Title page, illustrations, and ornaments by William A. Dwiggins; printed by Abbey Press. No. 129 of 1200. 24.1 × 16.1 cm.

134 Some Books on Printing and Design

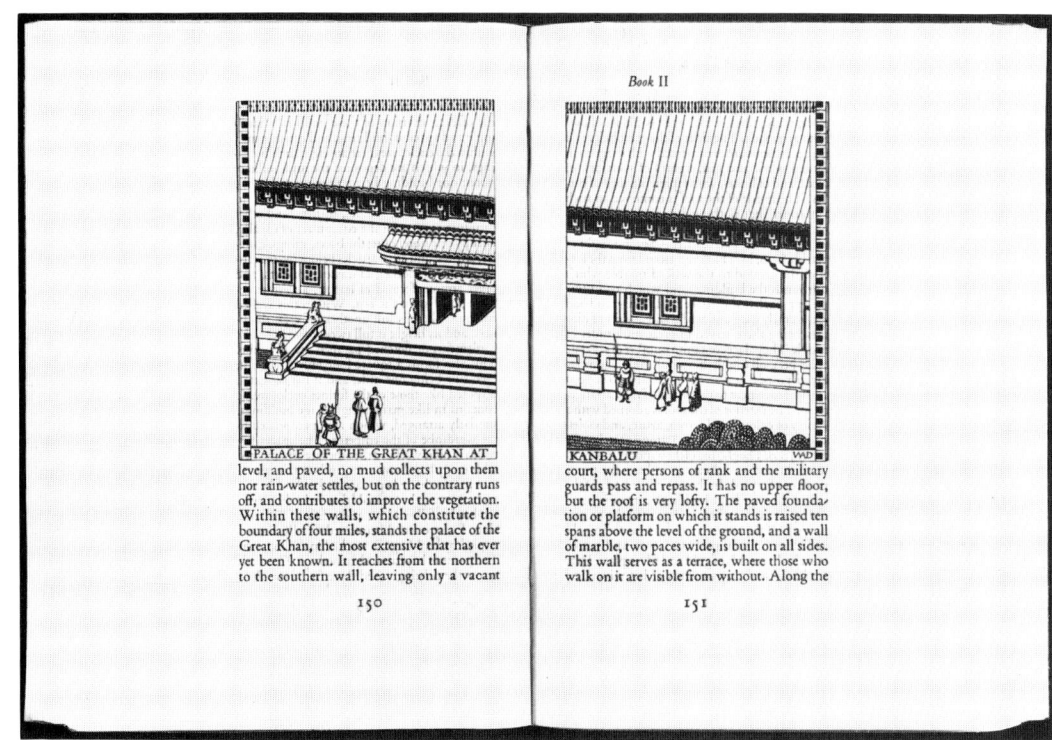

PLATE 80

PLATE 81

PLATE 82

PLATE 83

combination of his calligraphic decorations contained within bold geometric frames. Seemingly mirror images of one another, each of these is unique, relying on repetitions of selected elements to build an almost perfect symmetry. [81]

Dwiggins's preference for balanced design was expressed in a more subtle way in the format for *Gulliver's Travels*. Rather than have his illustrations span facing pages as in *Marco Polo* and *The Time Machine*, Dwiggins placed the illustrations on one page and matched their height and width to that of the text on the opposite page. The internal symmetry of the illustrations is en-

82. Jonathan Swift. *Travels into Several Remote Nations of the World of Lemuel Gulliver.* Mount Vernon, New York: Peter Pauper Press, [194–]. Illustrations, initials, ornaments, type, and book design by William A. Dwiggins. 25.8 × 16.5 cm.

83. *The Annual of Bookmaking, 1927–1937.* New York: The Colophon, 1938. Binding design by William A. Dwiggins. 27.9 × 19.5 cm.

forced throughout the book with vignettes at the top and bottom of each image. These same tiny landscapes are repeated with every illustration. [82]

The design of Dwiggins's bookbinding for the *Annual of Bookmaking* (1938) is an effective projection of his decorative style into a subtle relief. The intricately embossed elements are heightened with the silver and black inks and the play of the large and small shapes of the ornament against the background of the book cover. [83] The striking design of the slipcase for *Left to Their Own Devices*, produced the same year, was prompted by the special nature

84. *Left To Their Own Devices.* New York: The Typophiles, 1938. Binding design by William A. Dwiggins. No. 156 of 190. 16 × 10.5 cm.

85. William A. Dwiggins. *WAD to RR—a letter about designing TYPE.* Cambridge, Massachusetts: Harvard College Library, Department of Printing and Graphic Arts, 1940. 28.7 × 22.7 cm.

PLATE 84

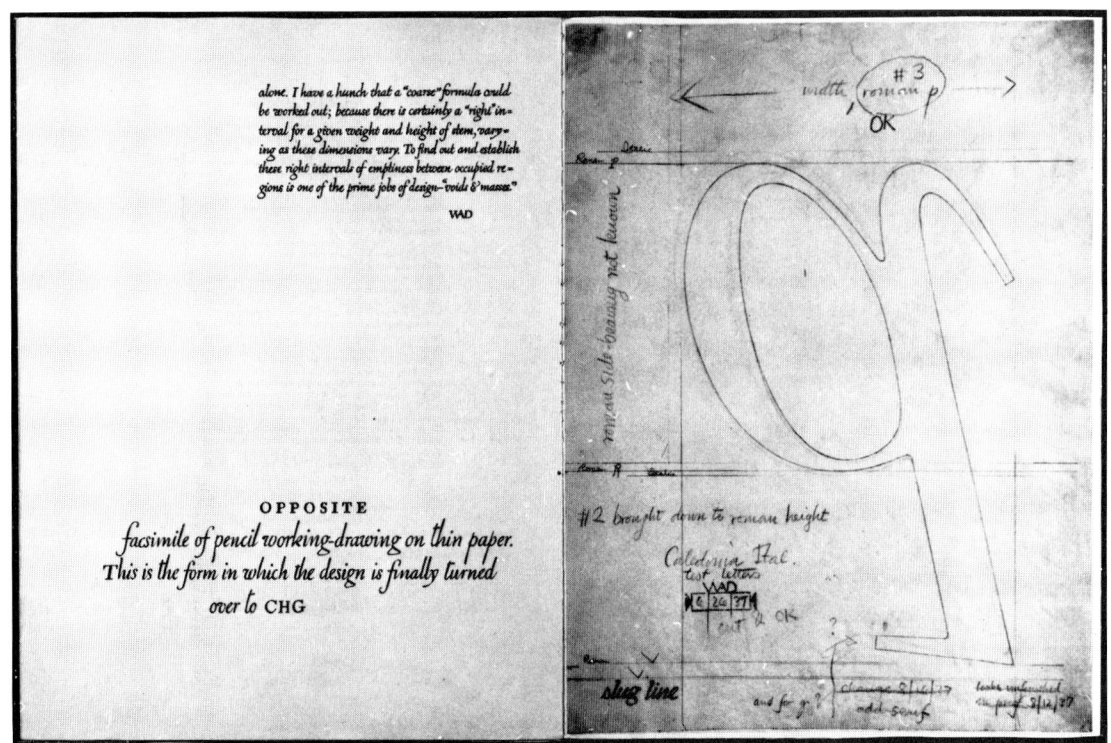

PLATE 85

of the book. It contains over one hundred pressmarks designed for the publisher by prominent American designers of the time. Dwiggins found it inappropriate to place one of his own distinctive marks on the cover. He solved his problem by simply labeling the slipcase with its contents, using the silk-screen technique to create the stenciled-letter effect. The result is disarming and precious, transforming the slipcase into a miniature shipping container. [84]

Dwiggins was also a designer of typefaces, including Electra, the type used in *Gulliver's Travels.* In *WAD to RR—a letter about designing TYPE* (1940), Dwiggins described to a friend the steps in creating a type design embroidered with comments on his personal approach. Subsequent to its publication Dwiggins recalled: "Somebody [said] to me: 'Singular book—all about making type, and yet there isn't a bit of type used in making it' . . . ." Reproduced photolithographically from Dwiggins's manuscript, the book contains a facsimile of a working drawing for one of his types. [85]

Some Self-advertisements

The best work by commercial printers is often seen in publications used to promote the services of a single company and in annuals celebrating the achievements of the trade. *The Annual of Advertising Art in the United States*, for instance, is a catalogue to a yearly exhibition of paintings and drawings created for advertisements. It first appeared in 1921, sponsored by The Art Directors Club, "to show forcefully that good art and good advertising are consistent and that successful advertisers are using as high a standard of art as that used in illustration or shown in the average exhibition of studio painting." Some of the illustrators and artists included in the exhibition were N. C. Wyeth, Joseph Pennell, Norman Rockwell, William A. Dwiggins, and Maxfield Parrish. [86]

The *Klimschs Jahrbuch*, begun in 1900, is an annual of graphic arts and processes, reporting on all aspects of the trade. The issue for 1932 contains over twenty articles including a review of *Jahrbuch* title page designs for the first thirty years, an essay on map printing, notes on new type designs, and surveys of new printing equipment. One new piece of equipment was the Selectasine-Schnellpresse, a high-speed silkscreen press. In addition to the usual specifications and descriptions of special fea-

86. *Annual of Advertising Art in the United States.* New York: The Art Directors Club, 1921. 29.1 × 20.6 cm.

87. *Klimschs Jahrbuch.* Vol. 25. 1932. Ed. by Konrad F. Bauer; published by Verlag von Klimsch. 27.6 × 20.1 cm.

142 Some Books on Printing and Design

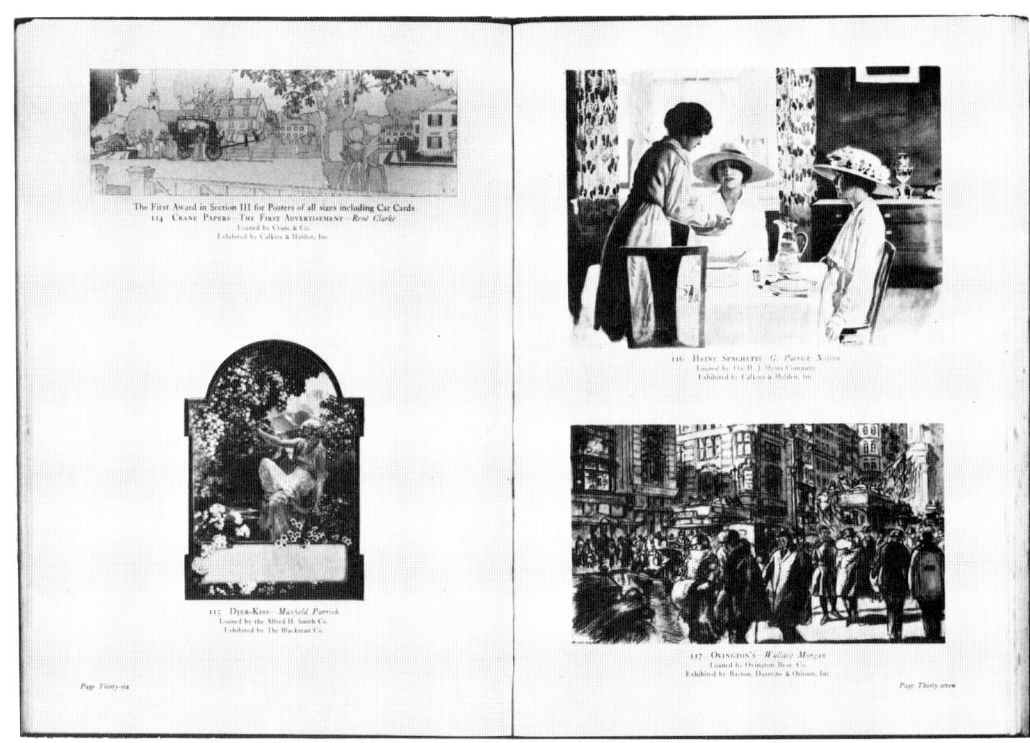

PLATE 86

Some Self-advertisements 143

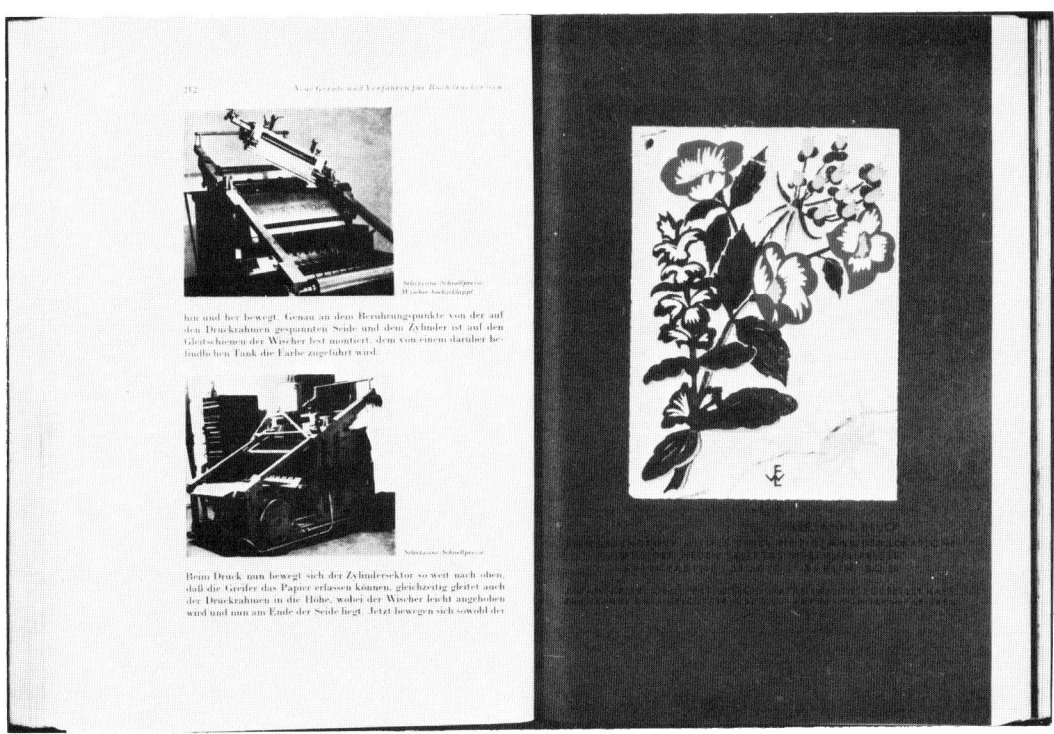

PLATE 87

tures, the article includes a sample printed by the press on Japanese paper. [87]

"The Biggest and Most Illuminating Exhibit of the Finest Examples of Photo-Engraving and Printing in America. . . ." With this announcement *Achievement in Photo-Engraving and Letter-Press Printing* was placed on sale in 1927. Estimated to be worth over seventy dollars, containing 870 pages, 645 full page illustrations, and weighing 11 pounds, the book was offered by its publisher, the American Photo-Engravers Association as

. . . . an example of co-operation and an outstanding public service on the part of a Trade Association . . . . It is essentially a collective effort and a work utterly impossible as a private enterprise conducted for profit. Price $10.00 per copy.

Achievement is an amazing feat of commercial cooperation in which the hundreds of separately produced illustrations are brought together to provide a unique view of the production capacity of an entire industry, from the best to the merely curious. The volume is opened to two pages of glassine candy-wrappers which pose a problem for printers. Glassine, which is coated to resist adhesion to foods and other substances, resists ink as well, particularly on a high-speed press. [88]

The Esselte Aktiebolag, a Swedish printing conglomerate, published *Grafiska Arbeten* (1937) as a sampler of its diverse services, including brochures, posters, magazine ads, maps, and a sample of graph paper. Small packaging, such as the foil-lined box for "Prinz Wilhelms Kaffe-Blandning," was a specialty of Esselte Aktiebolag. Be-

88. *Achievement in Photo-Engraving and Letter-Press Printing*. Ed. by Louis Flader. Chicago: American Photo-Engravers Association, 1927. 32 × 24 cm.

Some Self-advertisements

145

PLATE 88

146 *Some Books on Printing and Design*

PLATE 89

sides printing and folding, the manufacture of the box required lamination and die cutting techniques, the combination of which has become a separate industry today. Some of the same production methods were used for the promotional prop on the preceding page, and although the subject is the same, the design of the self-supporting display suggests a different client. [89]

89. *Grafiska Arbeten.* [Stockholm:] Esselte Aktiebolag, 1937. 34 × 27.5 cm.

Advertising Brochures

The advertiser who has turned to the format of promotional brochures expects from the printer a product which is not bounded by the limitations of size, printing techniques, and quality imposed by the commercial pages of periodicals. Accordingly, a printer's resources must be applied in imaginative ways in order to give expression to the advertiser's message.

Brochures for Bugatti and Renault illustrate two opposing advertising strategies in the automobile industry. The stark design of the Bugatti pamphlet is based on black-and-white illustrations, blueprint-style diagrams, and lists of engineering specifications printed with photolithographic and letterpress processes. It recommends the Bugatti to prospective buyers concerned with mechanical performance. [90] The Renault portfolio, on the other hand, epitomizes luxury, expressed by the soft, silver-over-white embossed cover. This mood is carried through the intimate arrangement in limp folders of loose four-color, photolithographic reproductions of an artist's muted renderings of the automobiles and passenger compartments. [91]

The expressionist drawing on the cover of *Die Stahlkirche* only hints at the interests of the publisher: the use of copper and copper alloys in building design. The sponsor, the Copper & Brass Research Association, was appealing to the aesthetic sensibilities of architects who would look

90. Automobile brochure for Bugatti. Place and date of publication unknown. Designed and printed by Fretz Frères. 23 × 16.1 cm.

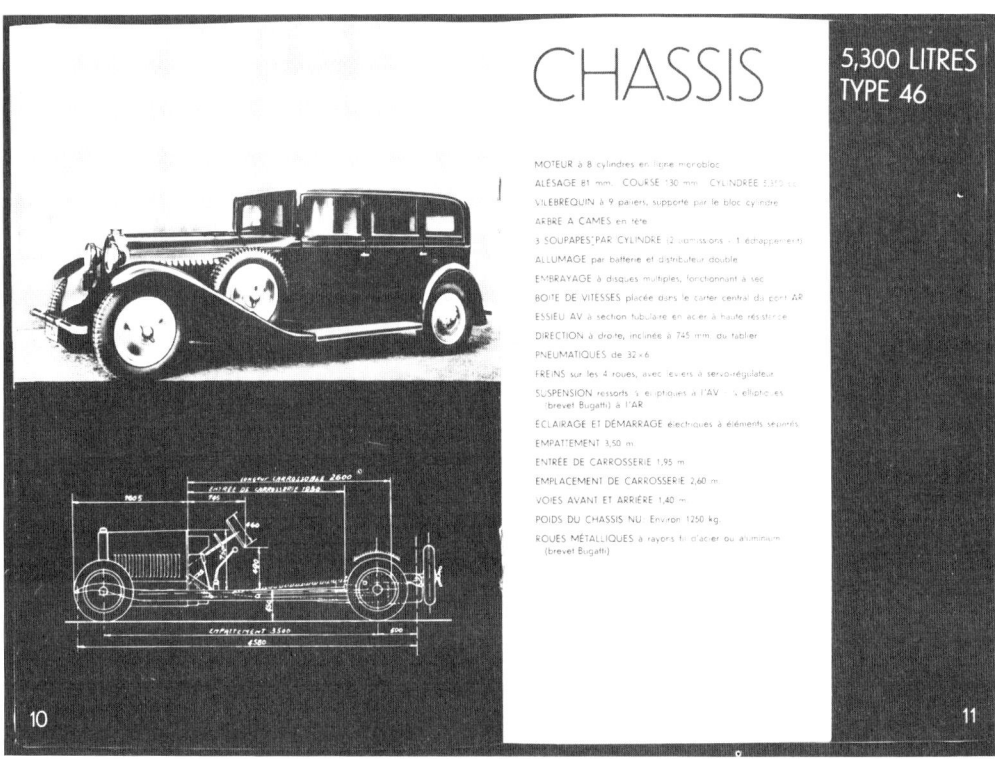

PLATE 90

critically at both the subject matter and its presentation. The cover is printed with the four-color, photolithographic process on a slightly textured paper to duplicate the surface of the artist's drawing. The views inside the brochure are printed on a calendered or polished paper suggestive of glossy photographs. [92, 93]

In 1931, the least expensive berth in a three-person cabin aboard the "Resolute's" round-the-world cruise was seventeen hundred, fifty dollars. No expense was spared in the production of *HAPAG Weltreise 1932*, a handsome promotional piece illustrated with maps, photographs, and schedules produced with three photomechanical printing techniques and four kinds of papers. The itinerary, which included stops in the Orient, is accompanied by two facsimile letterpress reproductions of Japanese and Chinese woodcuts. Printed on rice papers which have been tipped into the book, these are tangible enticements to the romance and mystery of distant shores. [94]

My Cunard Trip, commissioned by the Cunard Line during the 1920s or 30s, is British artist and travel-author Alexander K. MacDonald's account of a transatlantic voyage and return on Cunard steamships. Unlike the *HAPAG Weltreise*, the only diversions on these routine trips back and forth across the North Atlantic were the luxurious facilities of the "Aquitania" and the "Berengaria," and the discreetly observed peculiarities of MacDonald's ship-

91. Automobile brochure for Renault. Place and date of publication unknown. Printed by Draeger. 24.5 × 21.9 cm.

92,93. Otto Bartning. *Die Stahlkirche*. New York: Copper & Brass Research Association, 1930. 28 × 22 cm.

94. *HAPAG Weltreise 1932*. Hamburg: Hamburg-Amerika Linie, 1931. 24.6 × 17 cm.

PLATE 91

152   *Some Books on Printing and Design*

PLATE 92

PLATE 93

PLATE 94

154　　Some Books on Printing and Design

PLATE 95

mates. Accordingly the production of the brochure plays on the mock-intimate nature of the author's narrative. This was accomplished by reproducing the inviting format of his travel diary in a life-size, four-color, photolithographic facsimile bound with a ribbon. [95]

95. A.K. MacDonald. *My Cunard Trip*. Place and date of publication unknown. 38 × 21.1 cm.

Children's Literature

The printing of children's literature poses a challenge of producing books which are attractively designed, durable, and inexpensive. Printers' responses range from the firmly utilitarian to the ingeniously impractical, but all with the hope of capturing the uncertain attention of the child.

In the early years of the U.S.S.R. the Soviet leadership began a program to accelerate education through the centralization and expansion of the country's presses. Children's literature was made a priority with the result that leading Soviet designers and authors were brought together to create books combining the latest trends in design with the educational theories and needs of the state. The books were printed hastily, often ignoring color alignment, on inexpensive papers, and in huge editions of two to three hundred thousand, to keep the costs down. Nevertheless, as this selection printed in the late 1920s and 1930s shows, the planners succeeded in creating a variety of engaging and provocative designs. This was partially due to the use of abstract art, which established a foothold in Russia prior to the Revolution, flourished before the purges, and found its way into the children's literature. [96] In particular, the technique of collage, scraps of printed matter assembled to create designs, was often used and reproduced as a common and whimsical feature. [97, 98]

At the same time the Soviets were trying to reduce the cost of children's books,

96. Ol'ga Deĭneko. *V oblakakh* [*In the Clouds.*] Moscow: OGIZ, Molodaia Gvardiia, 1931. Illustrations by the author. 23 × 19.5 cm.

Children's Literature

PLATE 96

the Germans were applying expensive printing techniques to transform the books into toys and educational games. *Rein und Raub* has a die-cut hole punched through the book and amusingly integrated into the picture on each page. [99] *Das Zauberboot* (1929), written and illustrated by Tom Seidmann-Freud (1892–1930), is a play book "influenced by the discoveries of child psychology which assign an active role to the child even when he is looking at pictures." Nearly every page gives the child something to turn or pull. The book is opened to a miniature stage and accompanying dialogues where it becomes possible to create a private theatre; the child need only pull

97. D. Shterenberg. *Chaĭ* [*Tea.*] Moscow: OGIZ, Molodaia Gvardiia, 1931. 22.5 × 19.5 cm.

98. M. Pankov. *Stroim dvigateli* [*We Build the Engines.*] Moscow: OGIZ, Molodaia Gvardiia, 1931. Illustrations by L. Popova and B. Nikiforov. 19.1 × 14.8 cm.

PLATE 97

Children's Literature

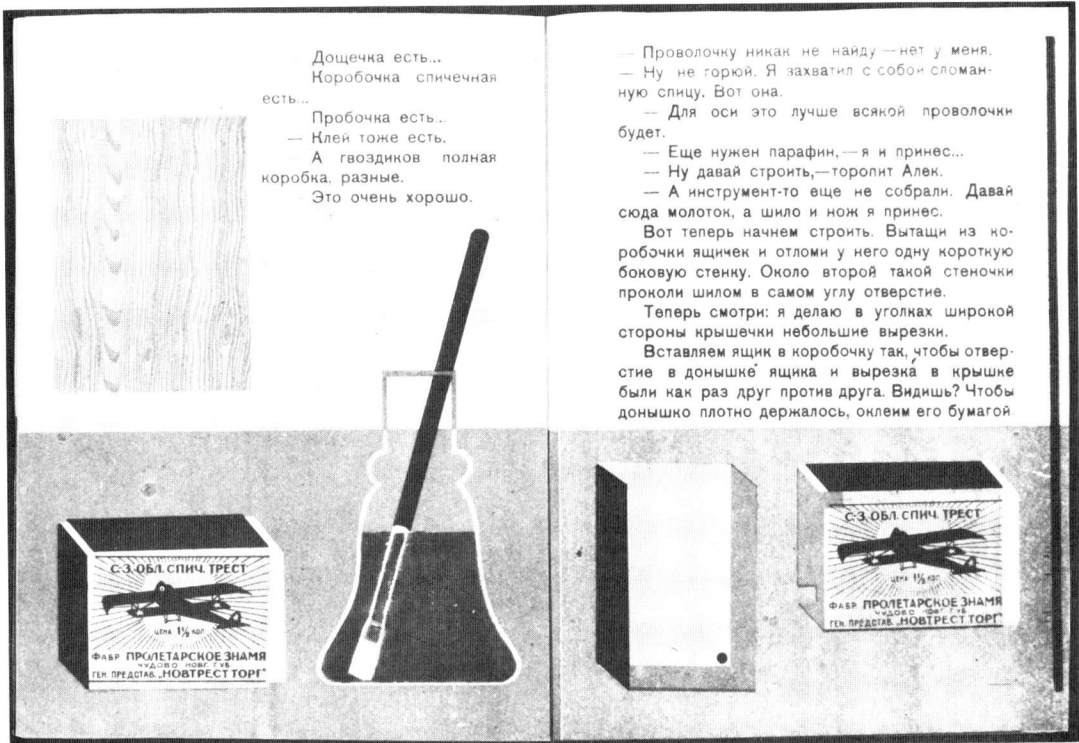

PLATE 98

PLATE 99

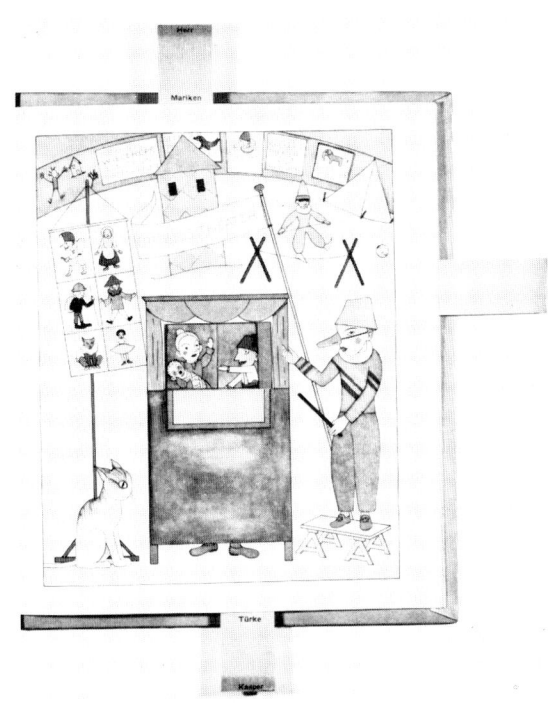

PLATE 100

the right-hand tab to open the curtain, and pull the other tabs to change the characters. However, the variety of loose parts and frail construction presume close parental supervision. [100]

The printing technique for the ultimate in practical book designs for young children—the cloth book—is serigraphy or stencil printing. *Le plus vieille histoire du monde* is printed with fabric dyes daubed through stencils designed by the artist. Since fabric can be dyed from one side only, each page of this book is actually one long piece of cloth with two images folded over

99. L.O. Peterson. *Rein und Raub: Eine lustige Mäusejage.* Mainz: Verlag Jos. Scholz, [n.d.] 22.3 × 18.5 cm.

100. Tom Seidmann-Freud. *Das Zauberboot: Ein Bilderbuch zum Drehen, Bewegen und Verwandeln (Das neue Wunderhaus).* Berlin: Herbert Stuffer Verlag, 1929. 24.1 × 20.9 cm.

162 Some Books on Printing and Design

PLATE 101

back-to-back. The subject is the Biblical creation story playfully told in words and pictures rendered by the artist Françoise Seignobosc. [101]

101. *Le plus vieille histoire du monde.* Paris: Jardin des Modes, [n.d.] Illustrations by Françoise Seignobosc. 21.5 × 25.7 cm.

Art and Photography

Interest in the *avant-garde* earlier in this century led to a number of magazines which kept abreast of the latest artistic developments by including original prints as well as photomechanical reproductions. This placed a special demand on printers. The artists represented within a single issue often worked in a variety of media requiring the integration of a number of hand-printing techniques with commercial processes.

The periodical *Byblis*, limited to editions of 500, published its first number in 1921. Featuring reviews of recently published artists' books and prints, *Byblis* also contained critical retrospective surveys of the graphic works of individual artists. Each issue was illustrated with original prints, as in this copy published in 1931, which includes lithographs, engravings, and these woodcuts by Raoul Dufy (1877–1953). Both of the woodcuts were reprinted especially for *Byblis*, the lower of the two taken from Dufy's first illustrated book, Guillaume Appolinaire's *Le bestiare ou cortège d'Orphée*, printed in 1911. [102]

Beginning in 1937, *Verve* brought together the work of many of the leading artistic and literary figures of the day including André Gide, James Joyce, Ernest Hemingway, Henri Matisse, Georges Braque, and Georges Rouault. Each issue contains photomechanical reproductions of art and photography, and original prints. These latter are sometimes arranged to highlight the work of an individual artist, or organized around a theme to show the works of several artists. The third issue includes a suite of original lithographs on the four seasons by the artists Marc Chagall,

Joan Miro, Abraham Rattner, and Paul Klee. It is opened to Chagall's contribution, titled "Spring." [103]

This period also witnessed the struggle by photographers to have their work recognized as an art form. Their success was due partially to a handful of high quality photography annuals made possible through the refinement of gravure, a technique based on photomechanically engraved metal plates. Gravure can maintain a highly detailed image for long press runs and deposit more ink on the paper, especially important in reproducing the extremely fine grain and deep, velvety blacks of photography. These reproductions are from two annuals important in the popularization of photography, *Das deutsche Lichtbild* which began in 1927, shown here in its 1931 issue, and *U.S. Camera* in its first number, published in 1935. [104, 105]

PLATE 102

PLATE 103

Art and Photography

102. *Byblis, Miroir des arts du livre et de l'estampe.* Vol. 37. 1931. Ed. by P.-J. Angoulvent. No. 89 of 500. 28.5 × 23 cm.

103. *Verve, An Artistic and Literary Quarterly.* Vol. 1, No. 3. 1938. Ed. by E. Tériade. 36 × 27 cm.

166　*Some Books on Printing and Design*

PLATE 104

Art and Photography 167

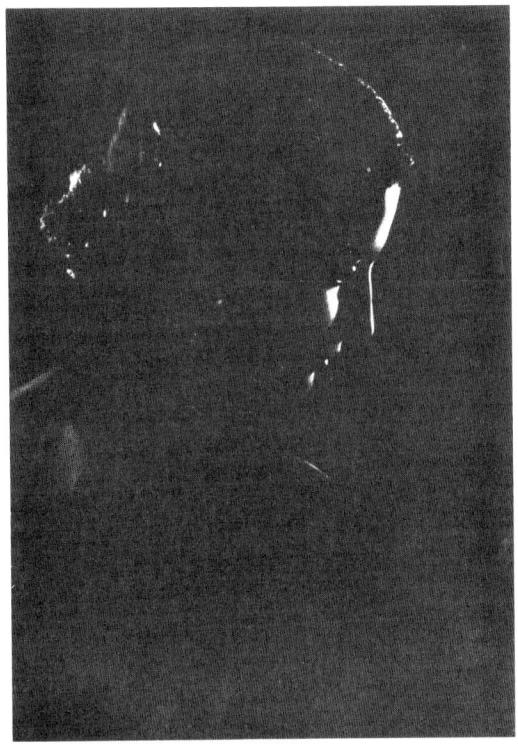

PLATE 105

104. *Das deutsche Lichtbild.* Berlin: Verlag Robert & Bruno Schultz, 1931. 28.5 × 23 cm.

105. *U.S. Camera.* Ed. by T. J. Maloney. New York: William Morrow & Company, 1935. 30.2 × 23 cm.

This catalogue was designed by Cynthia Susmilch and typeset and printed by the University of Chicago Printing Department. The italic and roman typefaces are Stempel Garamond, a twentieth-century modification of the early sixteenth-century designs of Claude Garamond. A computerized cathode ray tube typesetter, the technology for which was developed in the 1960s, was used to set the text. The catalogue was printed by offset lithography, an early twentieth-century adaptation of Senefelder's method to a rotary press.

The bookplate was designed for R. R. Donnelley & Sons Company by William A. Dwiggins. It is one of a number of pressmarks and bookplates created for the company by such prominent American illustrators as H. C. Leyendecker (who designed the first Indian-head motif in 1897), Rudolph Ruzicka, T. B. Hapgood, and Rockwell Kent.